Ambrose Bierce
Is Missing

Ambrose Bierce Is Missing

And Other Historical Mysteries

JOE NICKELL

THE UNIVERSITY PRESS OF KENTUCKY

Copyright © 1992 by The University Press of Kentucky

Scholarly publisher for the Commonwealth,
serving Bellarmine College, Berea College, Centre
College of Kentucky, Eastern Kentucky University,
The Filson Club, Georgetown College, Kentucky
Historical Society, Kentucky State University,
Morehead State University, Murray State University,
Northern Kentucky University, Transylvania University,
University of Kentucky, University of Louisville,
and Western Kentucky University.

Editorial and Sales Offices: Lexington, Kentucky 40508-4008

Library of Congress Cataloging-in-Publication Data

Nickell, Joe.
    Ambrose Bierce is missing and other historical mysteries / Joe
Nickell.
        p.   cm.
    Includes bibliographical references and index.
    ISBN 0-8131-1766-6
    1. History—Miscellanea.   2. Curiosities and wonders.   I. Title.
D21.3.N53   1991
902—dc20   91-3049

This book is printed on acid-free paper meeting
the requirements of the American National Standard
for Permanence of Paper for Printed Library Materials. ♾

Dedicated to
JOHN T. SHAWCROSS

Contents

Acknowledgments

Portions of this book first appeared in the author's doctoral dissertation, *Literary Investigation: Texts, Sources, and "Factual" Substructs of Literature and Interpretation*, University of Kentucky, 1987. I am supremely grateful to the members of my dissertation committee—John T. Shawcross (director), R. Gerald Alvey, John Greenway, Michael Harris, Jerome Meckier, and Rupert Pickens—for their help.

I also wish to thank the following publications for permission to reprint several articles, which appeared in somewhat different form under the titles given: *Skeptical Inquirer* (editor, Kendrick Frazier) for "The Nazca Drawings Revisited" and "Unshrouding a Mystery: Science, Pseudoscience, and the Cloth of Turin"; *Lincoln Herald* (editor, Joseph E. Suppiger; Scott D. Millar, executive vice president, Lincoln Memorial University), for "Lincoln's Bixby Letter: A Study in Authenticity"; *Filson Club History Quarterly* (editor, Nelson Dawson) for "Uncovered—the Fabulous Silver Mines of Swift and Filson" and "Daniel Boone Fakelore"; and *Free Inquiry* (editor, Paul Kurtz; managing editor, Mary Beth Gehrman) for "Mechanic of Death: The Case of Ivan the Terrible."

In addition to those individuals mentioned in the text I am also grateful to Robert H. van Outer and the University of Kentucky Photographic Services for photographic assistance; the staffs of the Margaret I. King Library, University of Kentucky, and the John F. Kennedy Memorial Library, West Liberty, Kentucky, for research assistance; my mother, Ella T. Nickell, for typing the manuscript; and the many others who helped in various ways, especially two who have since passed away—my father, J. Wendell Nickell, and my great uncle, Milton C. Nickell—with whom I spent much fondly remembered time in historical pursuits.

1 *Introduction*

History and the Investigative Approach

Man's view of history—the world's significant past events—does not remain static. Just as science came to discredit the theory of geocentricism (the belief that the earth is the center of the universe) and to acknowledge the truth of reports that stones fell from the sky, so it is with historiography (the writing of history):[1] One generation's dubious legend may become another's accepted historical fact—and vice versa.

Take ancient Troy, for example. That citadel of Asia Minor had been made famous by Homer's epic poem, *The Iliad*, which related how the Greeks besieged Troy to rescue the beautiful Helen. Later pseudochronicles helped diffuse the legend of the Trojan War throughout western Europe. There even arose a patriotic tradition, lasting for a millennium, that the dispersed heroes of the tale had founded such Western nations as England and France.[2] By the nineteenth century, however, most scholars had come to dismiss the tale of the Iliad—and with it the city of Troy—as mere fiction.[3]

Now the view has again changed, owing in part to the archaeological investigations of Heinrich Schliemann and others. In the 1870s Schliemann, a self-taught scholar, excavated what is now generally believed to be the fabled fortress of Troy. On the basis of much additional data—notably evidence that Troy *was* apparently sacked by invading Greeks about the twelfth or thirteenth century B.C.—the skeptical attitude toward the epic tradition has considerably softened.[4]

Schliemann had set out with a determination to uncover evidence of Homer's ancient world. His success was fabulous: In addition to the legendary city, he discovered—across the Aegean Sea in Greece—royal graves with astonishing riches. His successful approach—which culminated in the unearthing of clear proof of the great culture we now know as Mycenae[5]—was essentially a dramatic, *investigative* one.

While the verbs *research* and *investigate* can be used interchangeably, and indeed may denote the same activity, the latter term connotes a particular type of scholarly or scientific examination or inquiry. Not only does investigation involve an attempt to bring information to light, but it implies a type of information that is particularly obfuscated. Thus we may speak of conducting paleontological research, but of investigating the "mystery" of the dinosaurs' extinction. When there may be a suggestion of deliberate obfuscation, as in the clandestine or even criminal activities of individuals, the term *investigate* may seem especially appropriate. Therefore, while we "research" the effects of smoking or the causes of economic growth, we "investigate" a diversion of funds or a homicide. In short, the systematic seeking of knowledge is research, the attempt to solve a specific mystery an investigation.

We may extend the distinction to the historical arena. Thus "historical investigation" is defined as that aspect of research in which appropriate methodologies are applied toward the resolution of historical conundrums. For example, whereas one might refer broadly to Revolutionary War research, one would doubtless speak of an *investigation* to determine whether some questioned battle actually took place. Again, one may conduct research toward the writing of an important figure's biography, but *investigate* an apparent secret in his or her life.

The results of historical investigation may solve cultural, political, biographic, or other enigmas, or may shed light on additional historical problems. While some of these results may become only footnotes to history, they obviate the need for further investigation, may open up new areas for study, and may enhance the interpretation of that which was already known.

Procedurally, just as with a problem in law or science, the investigation of a historical mystery may involve several potentially applicable hypotheses. As David Binder and Paul Bergman state in their legal text, *Fact Investigation: From Hypothesis to Proof,* "Investigation is often all too readily thought of as merely a time to learn evidence. But remember that the evidence-gathering phase of investigation is normally preceded by analysis which ultimately dictates what evidence one pursues. This analysis concerns in part the potential legal theories and factual hypotheses that one may pursue during investigation."[6] Additionally, W.I.B. Beveridge—in his *The Art of Scientific Investigation*—describes the significance of hypothesis in investigation: "Hypothesis is the most important mental technique of the investigator, and its main function is to suggest new experiments or new observations. Indeed, most experiments and many observations are carried out with the deliberate object of testing an hypothesis. Another function is to help one see the significance of an object or event that otherwise would mean nothing. For instance, a mind prepared by the hypothesis of evolution would make many more significant observations on a field excursion than one not so prepared. Hypotheses should be used as tools to uncover new facts rather than as ends in themselves."[7]

The goal of the investigator—who abandons or modifies hypotheses as necessary—is the development of proof, in favor of one hypothesis, that is sufficient to solve the original problem. The standard of proof or persuasion required to settle historical questions has not been codified but can be characterized by analogy to the two standards used in civil law.

The lower standard (equivalent to "a preponderance of the evidence" in civil cases) would be represented in historical matters by the establishment of *the preferred hypothesis.* Basically, this would mean arriving at the one hypothesis, among those that can be advanced, which appears to account for all the evidence or at least which explains more data than do competing hypotheses.

When more than one hypothesis can account for the known facts, the preferred hypothesis can be determined by invoking "Occam's razor." Named for William of Ockham, the influential fourteenth-century philosopher, this principle affirms that the simplest explanation—that is, the hypothesis with the fewest assumptions—is most likely to be correct and is to be preferred.[8]

The second, or higher standard of persuasion would be comparable to that termed "clear and convincing evidence" in civil law. (The highest legal standard—required in criminal cases and known as "proof beyond a reasonable doubt"—would seem impractical for historical questions, although such a standard might well be achieved.)[9] Such a higher standard would of course involve evidence of a weight significantly greater than that sufficient to establish a preferred hypothesis. In general, the "clear and convincing" standard would apply to a hypothesis that had been rigorously tested (scientifically or critically) or could otherwise be upgraded to the status of accepted "theory."[10] Yet, as Martin Gardner cautions (albeit in a scientific context), "there are no known methods for giving precise 'probability values' to hypotheses."[11]

In any case, either the "preferred hypothesis" or the accepted theory may yet have flaws or leave some questions unanswered, so the mere raising of objections will be insufficient to remove it from its advantaged position. As Binder and Bergman state, regarding legal matters, "In most cases, despite the fact that the plaintiff has the burden of proof, both plaintiffs and defendants present affirmative as well as rebuttal evidence."[12] (In historical disputes, substitute "advocate of the new idea" for "plaintiff," and for "defendant" read "challenger of the assertion.") Therefore, it would seem appropriate that removal of a hypothesis or theory from its preferential position should come through development of a demonstrably superior hypothesis that would itself achieve advantaged status. Of course, evidence clearly fatal to a hypothesis or theory would cause its removal even in the absence of a replacement.

Another cautionary note regarding hypotheses involves bias, and Beveridge urges "the intellectual discipline of subordinating ideas to facts." As he explains: "A danger constantly to be guarded against is that as soon as one formulates an hypothesis, parental affection tends to influence observations, interpretation and judgment; 'wishful thinking' is likely to start unconsciously." He adds, "The best protection against these tendencies is to cultivate an intellectual habit of subordinating one's opinions and wishes to objective evidence and a reverence for things as they really are, and to keep constantly in mind that the hypothesis is only a supposition."[13]

The "wishful thinking" Beveridge warns against can even lead to a hypothesis being imposed on the data. A case in point is a 1982 article that attempts to identify Sir Arthur Conan Doyle, the creator of Sherlock Holmes, as the perpetrator of the Piltdown Skull hoax. Ignoring the considerable prima facie evidence pointing to Charles Dawson—who not once but twice "discovered" sets of the doctored bones and was otherwise linked to the hoax—the writer seems to have arrived at Conan Doyle by drawing his name out of a hat. Having once done so, however, he manages to marshal numerous insinuations and innuendoes as supposed evidence for his notion: Conan Doyle lived near the gravel pit where the bones were discovered (and hence could have planted them); he had a special knowledge of skulls; and so forth.[14] In sum, the article seems a classic example of starting with the answer and working backward to the facts.

Apart from such general guidelines for the formulation of hypotheses and the avoidance of bias, it is difficult to specify investigatory procedures. Even cases falling within the same general investigative area, and even having similar goals, probably require such different approaches as ultimately to have little in common from an investigative standpoint. For example, instances of biographical research—say the attempt to identify a nineteen-century politician's mistress, and the search for clues to a sixteen-century king's place of birth—would doubtless require investigative methodologies with little resemblance to each other.

Nevertheless, by recognizing some of the various divisions—or investigative *genres*—of the field of historical investigation, it is possible to gain an understanding of the types of problems each entails, together with some of the distinctive methodologies and standards of proof that have been applied in the past. That is the scope and purpose of the following chapters which focus on these major areas: ancient riddles, biographical enigmas, hidden identity, "fakelore," questioned artifacts, suspect documents, lost texts, obscured sources, and scientific challenges. Each chapter begins with an introduction to the specified area, follows with brief abstracts of typical cases that apply to it, and consists largely of an illustrative problem investigated by the writer.

These areas comprise a limited list; they can be easily divided and multiplied. The cited cases and illustrated methodologies are likewise only selections. Still, the chapters should be sufficient to characterize the field of historical investigation, provide some criteria for consideration, and perhaps suggest some specific approaches or even inspire the creation of new ones.

Recommended Works

The American Historical Association's Guide to Historical Literature. New York: Macmillan, 1961. A bibliography of 20,000 published works in history and related fields, selected and annotated; useful sourcebook for the historical investigator.

Binder, David A., and Paul Bergman. *Fact Investigation: From Hypothesis to*

Proof (St. Paul: West, 1984). A legal text that discusses such matters as gathering evidence, formulating a hypothesis, and developing proof.

"Historiography and Historical Methodology." *Encyclopaedia Britannica*, 1980, Macropaedia 8: 945ff. A concise, readable discussion of how the writing of history has changed over the centuries.

Stevenson, Noel C. *Genealogical Evidence: A Guide to the Standard of Proof Relating to Pedigrees, Ancestry, Heirship and Family History.* Laguna Hills, Calif.: Aegean Park Press, 1979. A standard work.

Winks, Robin W., ed. *The Historian as Detective.* New York: Harper and Row, 1969. Indispensable textbook for the historical investigator, featuring essays on evidence, biography, lost manuscripts, etc. Case studies include the Kennedy assassination, the Dead Sea Scrolls, and many more.

The Mystery
of the Nazca Lines

Mysteries beckon from the distant past. Time has typically obscured the contexts, erased the links, removed the ancillary evidence that would allow us to comprehend ancient events fully.
What remain are fragments, pieces of puzzles to be solved.

Often that is quite literally the case. Archaeologists expend
much time in assembling pottery shards, sifted and sorted from an
ancient site, into restored pots and other artifacts—rather like working jigsaw puzzles in three dimensions. From such restored jars,
bowls, or other items, the archaeological detective can identify a
particular culture, since each is characterized by its own distinctive
style of workmanship.[1]

Sometimes ingenuity enables the investigator to salvage that
which would otherwise be lost. For example, Sir Leonard Woolley, a
British archaeologist, was excavating at the biblical site of Ur of the
Chaldees when he discovered a small golden cap, like that which
might have covered the end of a wooden staff. Indeed, beneath the
cap was a cylindrical cavity left where some wooden object had
decayed. Peering into the small cavity, Woolley could see nails
crossing the space. If he dug up the area, he would risk destroying
the relationship that existed between whatever pieces of the unknown artifact remained.

Instead, Woolley carefully poured plaster of Paris into the cavity
until it was filled to the brim. After the plaster had hardened, he
carefully dug out the casting. Complete with shell inlay and a gold-
and-lapis bull's head decoration, the mysterious object was now
revealed as a queen's harp. (Further excavation yielded the remains
of ten women, all wearing elaborate headdresses of gold and car

nelian. The bones of one woman's hand had actually lain across the area where the harpstrings had once been.)[2]

On a larger scale, in another investigation, Woolley deduced a pattern from various clumps of weeds that sprouted from a gravel field near an old Hittite city in northern Syria. By digging beneath first one clump and then another and another, Woolley uncovered an ancient cemetery.[3] (Archaeologists frequently use such visual cues—subtle depressions, mounds, patterns of vegetation, and the like—to locate other hidden sites. Sometimes aerial photographs, taken early or late in the day when the low sun casts lengthy shadows, will show features that would otherwise go undiscovered.[4] Even *infrared* aerial photography has been successfully employed to reveal traces invisible to the unaided eye.[5])

Special investigative strategies have been developed for determining even great and complex patterns. In the early 1860s, for example, Edouard Lartet formulated a method for systematically tracing the changing fortunes of Old Stone Age man in Europe: "The answer must lie, he emphasized, in stratification—in the simple fact that any one layer of occupation debris must be older than the layer above and younger than the layer below. Once a sequence had been established by this method at any one site, it could be extended to others where artifacts of the same type were found in association with the bones of the same fauna. And in that way a gradually extending sequence could be worked out which eventually could cover the whole extent of the Old Stone Age."[6]

Other nineteenth-century prehistorians addressed another ancient mystery. It concerned megalithis ("great stone") monuments that were scattered in a sweeping belt along Europe's Atlantic coast. These monuments had long been the subject of speculation as to their origin and purpose. Were they—as was said of the most impressive of them, Stonehenge—transported in a wondrous manner by Merlin the magician? Were they associated with an early race of giants?[7]

The investigators attempted to synthesize the data gleaned by previous researchers. Excavated graves helped show that many of the megalithic structures were communal tombs, "and that the vast majority of the other jumbled megalithic monuments were the more or less ruined remains of similar structures, robbed of the soil and stones that had once covered them."[8] As to Stonehenge, notions that it had been a Roman or Druidic temple yielded to evidence that it dated from a much earlier time. It apparently underwent three phrases of development, from the Late Neolithic Period to the Early Bronze Age, as confirmed by considerable evidence including pottery shards and radiocarbon dating of charcoal taken from one of a ring of outlying holes.[9] (Carbon dating compares radioactive carbon-14, which breaks down at a known rate, with the stable isotopes of carbon. By this means, ancient *organic* materials—wood, cloth, and other carbon-based materials—can be dated to an accuracy of about a century of so.[10])

Most authorities believe Stonehenge was built as a place of worship. The fact that the latest phase (represented by a circle of upright stones capped by a ring of lintels) is aligned upon the sunrise of the summer soltice, has suggested the monument was a temple for sun worship. In more recent years, an astronomy professor used a computer to study various alignments of the sun and moon and concluded Stonehenge was a solar-lunar "observatory." This has become a popular view, but many scholars still urge caution.[11]

Other mysterious megaliths—great stone heads—flank the coastal area of a tiny, isolated isle in the Pacific, Easter Island. According to one source, "At first the carving and erecting of these monuments seem a more grandiose project than people with only stone tools and their own muscle power could have accomplished. So a number of theories have been propounded to account for them. They represent the remnants of a vanished civilization, perhaps even Atlantis; or they were built by extraterrestrial visitors; or the early islanders possessed the secret of antigravity, and simply *willed* the statues to move."[12] Archaeological investigation, however, together with scholarly interrogation of the present-day islanders plus some practical experimentation, has solved many of the fundamental questions about the strange effigies.

According to tradition, the island was populated by a chief and his followers who were forced to flee their homeland—reportedly one of the Marquesas Islands where the language and types of artifacts are similar. The curious statues were erected at various religious sites (called *ahu*) to honor respected ancestors.[13]

An open quarry, where statues are found in various states of completion along with discarded tools, provides detailed evidence of how the statues were created. Despite the assertions of writers like Erich von Däniken, who maintain the natives could not have moved the large statues,[14] experimenters have shown otherwise: how a simple bipod (an inverted *V* made of logs) with ropes could be used to "walk" a statue a few inches at a time; and how men with a lever could raise a statue a few inches, with rocks then being tossed underneath and the process repeated.[15]

Another ancient riddle has many of the elements we have discussed thus far: puzzling effigies, rendered fully visible only by aerial viewing, and mysterious as to their purpose; clues to the culture that made them provided by pottery and carbon-14 dating; and the need for experimentation to clarify important issues. This is the case we now treat at length, the mystery of the Nazca markings.

Called "Riddles in the Sand"[16] they are the famous Nazca lines and giant ground drawings etched across thirty miles of gravel-covered desert near Peru's southern coast.

The huge sketchpad came to public prominence in Erich von Däniken's *Chariots of the Gods?*—a book that consistently underestimates the abilities of ancient "primitive" peoples and assigns many of their works to visiting extraterrestrials. Von Däniken argues that the Nazca lines and figures could have been "built according to instructions from an aircraft."[17]

Von Däniken envisions flying saucers hovering above and beaming down instructions for the markings to awed primitives in their native tongue. He views the large drawings as "signals"[18] and the longer and wider of the lines as "landing strips."[19] But would extraterrestrials create signals for themselves in the shape of spiders and monkeys? And would such "signals" be less than eighty feet long (like some of the smaller Nazca figures)?

As to the "landing strip" notion, Maria Reiche, the German-born mathematician who for years has mapped and attempted to preserve the markings, has a ready rejoinder. Noting that the imagined runways are clear of stones and that the underlying ground is quite soft, she says, "I'm afraid the spacemen would have gotten stuck."[20]

It is difficult to take Von Däniken seriously, especially since his "theory" is not his own and it originated in jest. Wrote Paul Kosok, the first to study the markings: "When first viewed from the air, [the lines] were nicknamed prehistoric landing fields and jokingly compared with the so-called canals on Mars."[21] Moreover, one cropped photo exhibited by Von Däniken showing an odd config-

Figure 1. Etched upon the Nazca plains in Peru are giant drawings like these. Their large size has fueled misguided speculation that they were drawn with the aid of "ancient astronauts" or by sophisticated surveying techniques, the secrets of which are lost.

uration "very reminiscent of the aircraft parking areas in a modern airport"[22] is actually of the knee joint of one of the bird figures.[23] (See Figure 1.) The spacecraft that parked there would be tiny indeed.

Closer to earth, but still merely a flight of fancy in my opinion, is the notion of Jim Woodman and some of his colleagues from the International Explorers Society that the ancient Nazcas constructed hot-air balloons for "ceremonial flights," from which they could "appreciate the great ground drawings on the pampas."[24]

The Nazca markings are indeed a mystery, although we do know who produced them—Von Däniken notwithstanding. Conceding that Nazca pottery is found in association with the lines, Von Däniken writes, "But it is surely oversimplifying things to attribute the geometrically arranged lines to the Nazca culture for that reason alone."[25]

No knowledgeable person does. The striking similarity of the stylized figures to those of known Nazca art has been clearly demonstrated.[26] In addition to this iconographic evidence must be added that from carbon-14 analysis: Wooden stakes mark the termination of some of the long lines and one of these was dated to A.D. 525 (plus or minus 80). This is consistent with the presence of the Nazca Indians who flourished in the area from 200 B.C. to about A.D. 600. Their graves and the ruins of their settlements lie near the drawings.[27]

The questions of who and when aside, the mystery of *why* the markings were made remains, although several hypotheses have been proffered. One is that they represent some form of offerings to the Indian gods,[28] another that they form a giant astronomical calendar or "star chart."[29] Still another suggestion (first mentioned by Kosok) comes from art historian Alan Sawyer: "Most figures are composed of a single line that never crosses itself, perhaps the path of a ritual maze. If so, when the Nazcas walked the line, they could have felt they were absorbing the essence of whatever the drawing symbolized."[30] Sawyer is correct in observing that most of the figures are drawn with a continuous, uninterrupted line. But there *are* exceptions, and it is possible that the continuous-line technique is related to the method of producing the figures, as we shall discuss presently.

In any case, these are only some of the hypotheses; whatever meaning(s) we ascribe to the Nazca lines and drawings must be considered in light of other giant ground-markings elsewhere. Even putting aside the Japanese and European ones—e.g., the White Horse of Uffington, England, which is known from as early as the twelfth century[31]—we are left with numerous ground drawings in both North and South America.

In South America giant effigies are found in other locales in Peru, for example, and in Chile, in the Atacama Desert.[32] Interestingly, the plan of the Incan city of Cuzco was laid out in the shape of a puma, and its inhabitants were known as "members of the body of the puma."[33]

Turning to North America, there is the Great Serpent Mound in Ohio and giant effigies in the American Southwest. In 1978, with the aid of an Indian guide, I was able to view the ground drawings near Blythe, California, in the Mojave Desert. Like the Nazca figures, the Blythe effigies are large and give the impression they were meant to be viewed from the air. Also in common with the Nazca figures, they were formed by clearing away the surface gravel to expose the lighter-colored soil. Yet, although they are thought to date from a much later period,[34] none of the Blythe figures matches the size of the largest Nazca drawings, and the human figures and horselike creatures are much cruder in form.

Certainly the Blythe and other effigies have no attendant Von Dänikenesque "runways"; neither do their crude forms suggest they were drawn with the aid of hovering spacecraft. And there is nothing whatever to warrant the assumption that they were made to be viewed by select native balloonists on aerial sorties.

It seemed to me that a study of *how* the lines were planned and executed might shed some light on the ancient riddle. English explorer and film-maker Tony Morrison has demonstrated that, by using a series of ranging poles, straight lines can be constructed over many miles.[35] (The long lines "veer from a straight line by only a few yards every mile," reports *Time*.)[36] In fact, along some lines, the remains of posts have been found at roughly one-mile intervals.[37]

By far the most work on the problem of Nazca engineering methods has been done by Maria Reiche. She explains that Nazca artists prepared preliminary drawings on small six-foot-square plots. These plots are still visible near many of the larger figures. The preliminary drawing was then broken down into its component parts for enlargement. Straight lines, she observed, could be made by stretching a rope between two stakes. Circles could easily be scribed by means of a rope anchored to a rock or stake, and more complex curves could be drawn by linking appropriate arcs. As proof, she reports that there are indeed stones or holes at points that are centers for arcs.[38]

But Reiche does not detail the specific means for positioning the stakes that apparently served as the centers for arcs or the end points of straight lines. In her book she wrote, "Ancient Peruvians must have had instruments and equipment which we ignore and which together with ancient knowledge were buried and hidden from the eyes of the conquerors as the one treasure which was not to be surrendered."[39]

Be that as it may, William H. Isbell suggests that the Nazcas simply used a grid system adapted from their weaving experience, a loom "establishing a natural grid within which a figure is placed." All that would be necessary, he observes, would be to simply enlarge the grid to produce the large drawings.[40]

However, as one who has used the grid system countless times

(in reproducing large trademarks and pictorials on billboards—
summer work during my high school and college years), I am
convinced the grid system was not employed. To mention only one
reason, a characteristic of the grid method is that errors and distor-
tions are largely confined to individual squares. Thus, the "condor"
drawing in Figure 1—with its askew wings, mismatched feet, and
other asymmetrical features—seems not to have been reproduced
by means of a grid.

Other, even less likely possibilities would be the plotting of
points by a traverse surveying technique (such as is used today to
plot a boundary of land) or by triangulation. Having some experience with both of these, I note that such methods depend on the
accurate measurement of angles, and there appears to be no evidence that the Nazcas had such a capability.

I decided to attempt to reproduce one of the larger Nazca
figures—the 440-foot-long "condor" in the center of Figure 1—
using a means I thought the Nazcas might actually have employed.
I was joined in the project by two of my cousins, John May and Sid
Haney. The method we chose was quite simple: We would establish
a center line and locate points on the drawing by plotting their
coordinates. That is, on the small drawing we would measure along
the center line from one end (the bird's beak) to a point on the line
directly opposite the point to be plotted (say a wing tip). Then we
would measure the distance from the center line to the desired
point. A given number of units on the small drawing would require
the same number of units—larger units—on the large drawing.

For this larger unit we used one gleaned by Maria Reiche from
her study of the Nazca drawings and approximately equivalent to
12.68 inches. For measuring on the ground, we prepared ropes
marked off with paint into these Nazca "feet," with a knot tied at
each ten-"foot" interval for a total length of 100 units. To aid in
accuracy in plotting on the ground we decided to employ a *T* made
of two slender strips of wood. With this we could ensure that each
measurement made from the center line would be at approximate
right-angles to the line.

My late father, J. Wendell Nickell, took charge of logistics—
including obtaining permission to use a suitable giant "drawing
board" (a landfill area in West Liberty, Kentucky, owned by Dr. C.C.
Smith) and securing the services of a pilot for the subsequent aerial
photography. Since we could not mark the lines by clearing gravel

Figure 2. The author connects a plotted-and-staked point to another with twine in reproducing one of the largest Nazca figures, the giant "condor." (Photo by John May.)

to expose lighter-colored earth, as the Nazcas did, we planned to simply mark them with white lime, as one marks a playing field. With the addition of my young cousin, Jim Mathis, and my eleven-year-old nephew, Con Nickell, our work crew of Indians was complete.

On the morning of August 7, 1982, the six of us assembled at the site and immediately began by laying out the center line. Some nine hours, one meal, and much ice water later, we had plotted and staked the last of 165 points and had connected them with twine (Figure 2).

Here, I think, we differed slightly from the Nazcas, for I seriously doubt they expended just over a mile of string (the total distance traversed by the outline). I rather suspect that they made their furrows (or at least preliminary scratched lines) as they progressed in plotting the various points. We could not do this, since rain threatened and would certainly obliterate our lines of powdered lime.

Figure 3. A duplication of the giant "condor" drawing made full size and utilizing only sticks and cord such as the Nazcas might have employed. The experimental drawing—possibly the world's largest art reproduction—is viewed here from just under 1,000 feet. (Photo by John May.)

Figure 4. The author standing inside the right claw of the "condor" reproduction shown in Figure 3. View is from a stepladder. (Photo by J. Wendell Nickell.)

The rains did come, and while no harm was done to our staked-out condor, large puddles (then more rain and still more puddles) prevented our completing our project for about a week. Finally, the ground had dried, the weather forecast was good, and the pilot was on standby. My father and I then spent much of one day marking the lines, finishing just in time to see the airplane circling. Jerry Mays, a skilled local pilot, then took John and me up in his Cessna for a preliminary look and the taking of photographs, which John accomplished at just under 1,000 feet.

As Figure 3 shows, our work was a success. *Scientific American* termed the drawing "remarkable in its exactness" to the original.[41] In fact the results were so accurate that we are convinced we could have easily produced a more symmetrical figure by this method. Thus it would seem—unless they employed an even simpler method of making the enlargement—that the Nazcas plotted considerably fewer points. That, coupled with mere visual estimation of right angles and less careful measurement (distances might simply be stepped off), we could account for the imperfections we observed.

It is often asserted that the Nazca drawings are recognizable only from the air. That is not quite true, certainly not of the smaller figures, such as the effigy of a fish, which is only 80 feet long.[42] Neither is it true of some drawings—attributed to the Nazcas' predecessors—that are found on hill slopes.[43] Here, seemingly, is a clue to how the Nazcas could have been confident of the accuracy of their method of enlargement. Once a technique was found to be successful for producing large drawings on slopes, where they could actually be viewed from the ground, the same technique could be expected to yield good results consistently—wherever figures were drawn and whatever their size.

Moreover, even the large drawings can be appreciated to some extent from the ground. With our condor, we were able to see whole portions—such as body and head, leg and foot, the entire fan of the tail (see Figure 4)—and thus had determined the figure was reasonably accurate even before our flyover. We felt that an observer would be able to recognize it as a bird.

To test this possibility, my father took wildlife biologist Harold Barber to the site. Although Barber knew nothing of our project, and Nazca was deliberately not mentioned, on viewing the figure he recognized the drawing as one of the Nazca birds.

In summary, we do know that it was the Nazcas who produced the drawings. While their large size does suggest the possibility that they were meant to be viewed from above, as by the Indian gods, the figures can be recognized, at least to some extent, from the ground. The drawings could have been produced by a simple method requiring only materials available to South American Indians centuries ago. The Nazcas probably used a simplified form of this method, with perhaps a significant amount of the work being done freehand. There is no evidence that extraterrestrials were involved. But if they were, one can only conclude that they seem to have used sticks and cord just as the Indians did.

Recommended Works

Bibby, Geoffrey. *The Testimony of the Spade.* New York: Knopf, 1956. A survey of Old World archaeological discoveries.

Deetz, James. *Invitation to Archaeology.* Garden City, New York: Natural History Press, 1967. An American Museum Science Book, published by the American Museum of Natural History, offering the general reader an authoritative view of all aspects of archaeology.

Mysteries of the Ancient World. Washington, D.C.: National Geographic Society, 1979. Popular view of several ancient archaeological mysteries: Troy, Easter Island, Stonehenge, Jericho, and others.

Robbins, Maurice, with Mary B. Irving. *The Amateur Archaeologist's Handbook*, Third Edition. Cambridge: Harper and Row, 1981. Thorough treatment of the subject—including planning excavations, conducting a "dig" and recording data, preserving and restoring artifacts, etc.—for the enthusiast; features a chapter on historical archaeology, valuable appendices, and numerous illustrations.

Ambrose Bierce Is Missing

Biography—or life history—is not only important in its own right, but it can also function as an essential element of a larger historical view. (How complete, for example, would be our comprehension of the Civil War without the attendant biographies of presidents Lincoln and Davis, of generals Grant and Lee?) In either case, an investigative approach is likely to return the greatest dividends.[1]

Even so, Leslie A. Marchand could scarcely have anticipated the wealth of unpublished biographical materials he would uncover when he set out across Europe in the late 1940s "following Byron's trail." They ranged from "innumerable boxes of Byroniana" still at the publisher's, to three little volumes discovered at a country bookseller's that proved to be notebooks of Byron's wife, to still further manuscript material located in Greece. In evaluating this newfound material over the next several years, Marchand found that it "fills in missing parts of the jigsaw puzzle or gives more meaning to what had to be guessed at before."[2]

In antithesis to Marchand's praiseworthy sleuthing is the muckraking approach to the life of Poe (1850) taken by literary scavenger Rufus W. Griswold.[3] The Reverend Griswold was an enemy of Poe who, after the writer's death, nevertheless became his literary executor and proceeded to blacken Poe's name out of vindictiveness. Yet Griswold's nefarious activities—including forgery—were exposed by the investigative work of the later Poe biographer, Arthur Hobson Quinn. Quinn also uncovered another who had contributed to the negative portrait, temperance advocate Dr. J.E. Snodgrass, whose accounts of Poe's death became increasingly embellished. As Quinn characterized such attacks. "Almost at the very minute when the sods were falling on Poe's coffin, the fingers of slander were reaching for his fame."[4]

Quite as bad as the unfair treatment of a Griswold is the flattering, mythologizing impulse of some biographers, among them Agnes Strickland, with her *Lives of the Queens of England* (in twelve volumes, 1840-49), and Washington Irving, with his *Columbus* (1828). The same impulse prompted a group of Lord Byron's friends and family representatives to burn the manuscript of his scandalous memoirs,[5] and some of Emily Dickinson's letters were similarly destroyed.[6]

Lyndon Johnson—who had what has been described as an "obsession with secrecy"—handled matters himself. He often penned "Burn this!" on letters just before mailing them. His instructions were generally carried out, but a witness to the practice, and at least one letter so marked, were uncovered by his biographer, Robert A. Caro,[7] who said that "the major problem in writing about Lyndon Johnson's early life was his desire for secrecy and concealment. He had a unique talent for it. I don't think many people would have gone to the trouble, as he did, of having pages of his college yearbook, which detailed unsavory episodes of his college career, cut out with a razor blade from hundreds of copies of the yearbook."[8] Caro concludes that Johnson "tried to write his own legend for history, and he almost succeeded."[9] Johnson—like many before and since—seems to have regarded the biography as (in the words of the seventeenth-and-eighteenth-century Scotch writer John Arbuthnot) "one of the new terrors of death."[10]

While to some extent any good biography will make use of an investigative approach, often there is some particular, mysterious aspect that invites concerted effort: For example, James G. Randall sifted the evidence pertaining to the alleged romance between Abraham Lincoln and Ann Rutledge, with the result that the authenticity of the story was demolished. (Ann was actually engaged to another man, John McNamar, and evidence for her alleged romance with Lincoln consisted solely of the reminiscences of very elderly persons collected after Lincoln's death.)[11]

Similarly, an investigation by radio broadcaster Fred Goerner focused on the fate of the famous aviatrix, Amelia Earhart, and her navigator, Fred Noonan, lost on a globe-circling flight in 1937. But evidence that supposedly showed the pair had gone down off course, and were captured by the Japanese, evaporated. (A photo of

Earhart, supposedly in handcuffs on the island of Saipan, was actually made in Honolulu and showed here wearing a common bracelet. Exhumed remains proved not to be those of her and Noonan. And "eyewitness" testimony led nowhere, as did recovered artifacts—including a direction finder—that were of Japanese rather than American manufacture.)[12] What had gone wrong? Goerner seems to have settled early on the thrilling Japanese capture scenario, and been unable to free himself of it. Less fanciful investigators have concluded the pair's Lockheed Electra plane probably became lost at sea.[13]

Many of the foregoing investigative approaches—following an author's "trail," ferreting out biographical bias or cover-up, and attempting to separate legend from fact—could all be required in a single, particularly difficult case, the mysterious disappearance of the American writer Ambrose Bierce.

In his collection of horror and mystery tales, *Can Such Things Be?* (1893), Ambrose Bierce included a trilogy of stories under the subheading, "Mysterious Disappearances." They are not mere tales of missing persons; instead, in each the disappearance has elements of the supernatural: a planter walking across his pasture disappears in full view of his wife and a neighbor; a runner stumbles in a footrace and vanishes before touching the ground; and a sixteen-year-old lad fails to return from an errand, whereupon his tracks are found to end abruptly in the snow.[14]

Bierce's own unsolved disappearance in late 1913 seems an altogether fitting end for a writer who was fascinated by "mysterious disappearances" to the extent that he apparently collected them and wrote three tales of that genre, who had become almost famous for his "obscurity," and who, as old age overtook him, began increasingly to long for "the good, good darkness."

Born in 1842, the son of an Ohio farmer, Bierce distinguished himself as a Union soldier in the Civil War, at the close of which he claimed to have been breveted a major. Subsequently he was a Treasury clerk in San Francisco. He began his journalistic career about 1868 as editor of the *News Letter* in San Francisco. In 1872 he went to London where he remained until September 1875, achieving a reputation as a humorist for his tales and fables which were collected in 1874 under the title, *Cobwebs from an Empty Skull*. The next several years were spent in San Francisco—where Bierce con-

Figure 5. American writer Ambrose Bierce in a photograph from the 1890s. (Department of Special Collections, Stanford University Libraries.)

tributed to such publications as the *Overland Monthly* and the *San Francisco Examiner,* and edited the *Argonaut and the Wasp*—and in 1900 he moved permanently to Washington. By then he had published additional collections of stories, and over the next decade still further ones, plus a collection of verse, a cynical lexicon (later know as *The Devil's Dictionary*), his "black list" of literary faults called *Write It Right,* and the first ten volumes of *The Collected Works of Ambrose Bierce* (see Figure 5).[15]

Bierce's disappearance occurred sometime late in 1913 or early the following year. His close friend and biographer, Walter Neale, discredits the popular legend that the elderly writer met his death while serving with Pancho Villa's forces in Mexico.[16] However, Neale stands all but alone on this matter.

Another Bierce biographer, C. Hartley Grattan—noting Bierce's failed marriage, the death of his son Leigh in 1901, and his abortive attempt at remarriage in 1910—writes: "In the fall of 1913 dissatisfaction came to a climax, and he planned a trip to Mexico and perhaps to South America. That he regarded it as the final phase of his life that would in all probability end in death there is little doubt. That he planned it as a melodramatic disappearance and suicide there is every doubt in the world. He simply preferred, if he must face death, to face it in action."[17] When Bierce had announced his intention to some New Jersey friends, it seemed final. As one recalled: " 'When you come back,' I said, 'come first to us and rest.' He did not answer; but after a little he said softly, 'When I come back . . .' and I saw him turn his face quickly away."[18]

Bierce put his affairs in order and began to write farewell letters to friends. They clearly reveal his attitude at the time, that his journey was to be a final one. Here, pieced together from these letters, is a composite last letter—a de facto suicide note, Neale would say—from Ambrose Bierce. (For optimum coherence, the chronology of statements has been slightly altered, but no editorial additions have been made.)

My Dear_____.
This is to say good-by at the end of a pleasant correspondence in which your woman's prerogative of having the last word is denied to you. Before I could receive it I shall be gone. My work is finished, and so am I.
. . . I am going away and have no notion when I shall return. I expect to go to, perhaps across, South America—possibly via Mexico. . . .
. . . If you hear of my being stood up against a Mexican stone wall and shot to rags please know that I think that a pretty good way to depart this life. It beats old age, disease, or falling down the cellar stairs. To be a Gringo in Mexico—ah, that is euthanasia!
You must try to forgive my obstinacy in not "perishing" where I am. Civilization be dinged!—it is the mountains and the desert for me.
Pray for me? Why, yes, dear—that will not harm either of us. I loathe religions, a Christian gives me qualms and a Catholic sets my teeth on edge, but pray for me just the same, for with all those faults upon your head (it's a nice head, too), I am pretty fond of you, I guess. May you live as long as you want to, and then pass smilingly into the darkness—the good, good darkness.
. . . Don't know where I shall be next. Guess it doesn't matter much.
Adios,
Ambrose.
P.S. you need not believe *all* that these newspapers say of me and my purposes. I had to tell them *something*.[19]

What Bierce told the newspapers is known only from a clipping he reputedly sent his niece in a letter of November 6, 1913. It says, in part:

Mr. Bierce was dressed in black. From head to foot he was attired in this color, except where the white cuffs and collar and shirt front showed through. He even carried a walking cane, black as ebony and unrelieved by gold or silver. . . .

"I'm on my way to Mexico, because I like the game," he said, "I like the fighting; I want to see it. And then I don't think Americans are as oppressed there as they say they are, and I want to get at the true facts of the case."[20]

Bertha Clark Pope, editor of *The Letters of Ambrose Bierce*, adds:

In December of that same year the last letter he is known to have written was received by his daughter. It is dated from Chihuahua, and mentions casually that he has attached himself unofficially to a division of Villa's army, and speaks of a prospective advance on Ojinaga. No further word has ever come from or of Ambrose Bierce. Whether illness overtook him, then an old man of seventy-one, and death suddenly, or whether, preferring to go foaming over a precipice rather than to straggle out in sandy deltas, he deliberately went where he knew death was, no one can say.[21]

However, word purporting to come from, or about, Ambrose Bierce has been considerable. There is, for example, the reported "execution" of Bierce by Mexican firing squad in 1915. This account, from the *Mexican Review,* claims "a former officer in the constitutionalist army" had met Bierce several times, last talking with him in the vicinity of Chihuahua in late 1913 or early 1914. The officer claimed he later met "a sergeant of Villa's army" who had "witnessed the execution of an American who corresponded in every manner with Bierce's description.[22]

The "execution"—ordered by Villa's bloodthirsty General Thomas Urbina—allegedly took place near the village of Icamole in August 1915. Bierce, the sergeant supposedly claimed, died along with a Mexican—both with unbandaged eyes, on their knees, and with arms outstretched. The pair were said to have been "buried by the side of the trail."[23]

Vincent Starrett rightly scoffs at this story. As he observes, "First, this is the only one of a great many stories despite its painstaking vraisemblance; and, second, the execution is dated in the fall of 1915, approximately two years after Bierce's last letter." Starrett insists that Bierce would surely have communicated with family and friends had he been alive during this time. "This is recognized by all who knew him best," states Starrett, "and is the final answer to the extravagant chronicle in the *Mexican Review*." [24]

Further elaboration on Bierce's "execution" appeared in 1920. Reportedly, Bierce had been military adviser to Carranza when he had been "captured." As proof that it had indeed been Bierce, a photograph was alleged to have been found on the "body." This had supposedly been in the possession of an Indian who subsequently destroyed it, fearing reprisals when the story was published. To the observation of a friend of Starrett's that the author of this story was "an old and reliable journalist," Starrett replied that "*if* he is reliable, he is extraordinarily gullible, whatever his age." [25]

Still another chapter in the Bierce apocrypha maintains that as late as five years after his last letter Bierce had been in the company of an Indian in San Luis Potosi. The Indian—who had known Bierce as "Don Ambrosio"—had, alas, been murdered, reports a skeptical Starrett. [26]

So the stories multiply. M.E. Grenander believes Bierce perished in the battle of Ojinaga on January 11, 1914. He cites one of General Ortega's officers who supposedly had seen Bierce going into battle, and another rebel officer who is said to have heard that "an old gringo" had been shot during the conflict. Although Grenander has "no doubt" this is what actually happened to Bierce, he concedes "the evidence is circumstantial." [27]

E.F. Bleiler is one who is skeptical of all such stories, including one that Bierce was murdered "in the dead of night" [28] because he had insulted Villa. Bleiler states, "The perpetual stories of Mexicans who remember the quarrel between Villa and Bierce, or Bierce's burial on the battlefield, invariably peter out into uncertainties when investigated." [29] Grattan adds, "If the number keeps on increasing as many Mexican towns will claim to have been the death place of Bierce as Grecian towns claimed to be the birthplace of Homer. There are three so far: Sierra Mojada, Icamole, and Chihuahua. The stories that cluster about these three towns have a resemblance to each other, but no one story has yet been authenticated." [30]

One of the most outrageous of the postdisappearance stories concerning Bierce found the aged writer in good health, in France, as an officer on Lord Kitchener's staff. This was reported in a dispatch to the *New York World*, dated April 3, 1915, from Bloomington, Illinois. The article avowed that Bierce's daughter, Mrs.

H.D. Cowden of Bloomington, had received a letter from her father clearing up the mystery of his disappearance. "Yet," responds Starrett, "from Mrs. Cowden's own lips I have had it that no such letter, no such information conveyed in whatever manner, had ever reached her." He adds, "This is all sensational journalism." [31]

Did Bierce actually go into Mexico? As apparent evidence that he did, there is the "last letter he is known to have written," cited by Bertha Clark Pope (above). However, she seems to be merely paraphrasing Vincent Starrett who wrote: "In December of 1913 the last letter he is known to have written was received by his daughter. It was dated the month of its receipt, and from Chihuahua, Mexico. In it Bierce mentioned, casually enough, that he had attached himself, unofficially, to a division of Villa's army—the exact capacity of his service is not known—and spoke of a prospective advance on Ojinaga. The rest is silence." [32] We note that both Pope and Starrett refer to this as Bierce's last letter; that it is to Bierce's daughter; that the exact date in December is not given; and that Bierce's attachment to Villa's forces is termed unofficial. Neither Pope nor Starrett gives any source for the text of this letter which they do not—we further observe—quote directly.

However, writing in 1929, C. Hartley Grattan states that Bierce "was next heard from [after the reported interview, given above] at Chihuahua, Mexico, from whence he sent his final messages to his family and friends. The specific cause of his writing was to acknowledge a draft that had been forwarded to him there from Washington by his secretary, Miss Christianson. After positively proving that he was in Chihuahua one can give nothing but speculations." Grattan gives no source for these additional "facts." And his misspelling of Miss Carrie Christiansen's name further suggests he may be a less than trustworthy source for this information. [33]

To all this Walter Neale states that while he never saw Miss Christiansen after Bierce's disappearance, they frequently wrote each other. In none of her letters, Neale says, did she so much as imply that she had heard from Bierce since she and the elderly writer had parted in Washington in mid-1913. Neale adds:

Simple analysis shows the improbability that she should be sending any one or more drafts to him. Was she to take the risk of reaching him in Mexico amid the turmoil of a revolution? What sort of mail service had Villa the bandit? Was she to reach Bierce by mail while he would be journeying astride a donkey across the trackless Andes?. . . . Furthermore Bierce had left Washington without supplying any forwarding address at the Army and Navy Club, where he received his mail, and left word at the club to return to the writers, unopened, all mail for him delivered at that address, where the names and addresses were known, and, where not known, to hand the letters to the postman as being unclaimed.[34]

Moreover, says Neale, although Bierce and Miss Christiansen shared a safety deposit box in Washington, Bierce took the keys with him when he left. Consequently, Miss Christiansen was forced to apply for a court order to allow her to have the box forced open. "If she had been in contact with Bierce," asks Neale, "why had he not returned the keys to her?"[35]

The most elaborate account, perhaps, of Bierce's supposed last letter comes from Paul Fatout (1951):

Later in November the traveler [Bierce] moved on to El Paso, where international relations were so friendly that crossing the border was comparatively simple. Moving across to Ciudad Juarez, Ambrose was cordially received and given credentials as an observer attached to Villa's army marching to Chihuahua. By November 28 he was some thirty miles south of Juarez, riding hard through hot days and being chilled by cold nights. The country was disrupted by revolution and counterrevolution. . . .

In late December he was just outside Chihuahua, expecting to move to Ojinaga, partly by rail. . . . The Gringo observer was regarded with some suspicion by the Mexicans, but he removed their doubts by calmly walking to the top of a ridge and picking off one of the enemy. Whereupon his delighted comrades, astonished at such sharpshooting, presented him with a sombrero in token of his acceptance as a soldier. The irony of the sworn foe of revolution winning the acclaim of revolutionists must have tickled his sardonic fancy.

Irony? Fancy? Or fiction. Fatout concludes, "He rode in four miles to Chihuahua to mail a letter that spoke of these and other matters, and that was dated December 26, 1913. The rest is silence." Note that Fatout also fails to quote Bierce directly or to say to whom this letter was addressed. Neither does he mention any draft forwarded to Bierce by Miss Christiansen (although that may be included under "other matters"). He alleges Bierce was "given credentials," which seems to contradict earlier sources that Bierce was attached "unofficially" to Villa.[36]

However, Fatout does give a source for his information, namely, "Bierce papers, the Stanford University Library." A search for the reputed letter of December 26, 1913, uncovered no such document. Carol Rudisell, manuscript librarian at Stanford, has informed me that Stanford positively does not have such a letter, nor is there any evidence that it had ever acquired the letter. She states she would be "surprised" if anyone had actually found the letter, "especially if they found it here."

However, the Stanford University Library owns a "notebook" or "diary" which is in Miss Christiansen's handwriting and which has an entry for such a letter (together with a brief description of its contents).[37] This is clearly the same notebook which (I later learned) was reproduced by Carey McWilliams in the *American Mercury* in 1931 (although with errors). McWilliams states that "Miss Christiansen destroyed the letters ([from Bierce], pursuant to instructions, but she wisely jotted down the facts in them in a notebook." The last entry reads as follows (including crossed-out words):

Chihuahua Mexico
     Dec. 26, 1913
Ridden in four miles to mail a letter. Ride from Juarez to Chihuahua hard—nights hot da cold, days hot. Allusion to Jornada del Muerta (journey of death) of thousands of civilian refugees, men, women and children. Train load of troops leaving Chihuahua every day. Expect (next day) to go to Ojinaga, partly by rail. Mexicans fight "like the devil"—though not so effectively as trained soldiers. Addicted to unseasonable firing, many times at random. Incident at Tierra Blance—Refuge behind a sharp ridge—Story of Gringo—present of sombrero

One can only remark at how conveniently Miss Christiansen both destroyed the "letters" and "wisely jotted down the facts." In any event, McWilliams accepted the notebook entries as true even though he quoted the former American consul in Chihuahua who had "investigated" Bierce's disappearance and "could find no evidence that Mr. Bierce had been in Chihuahua."[38]

While there may not be conclusive proof that Bierce did *not* go to Mexico, there certainly seems less than adequate proof that he did. Moreover, as Neale writes, "At the time Bierce disappeared he had not been on a horse for many years. I wonder how long he, in his old age, could have remained on the back of one of Villa's bucking bronchos? The serenity of his latter years was not to be broken at the age of seventy-two by anything but asthma, of which he always stood in dread, and which the romancers would have us believe he courted in Mexico."[39] Neale argues against the "more fanciful of the journalists" who had suggested Bierce had been serving with Villa's forces when he met his death. Neale notes that Bierce had "roundly denounced Villa time and again throughout that bandit's stormy career," and that Bierce's sympathy, in fact, was entirely with the Carranzistas whom he had upheld and given his moral support. Neale adds, "That Bierce could have become a member of Villa's rabble band is unthinkable."[40]

Yet if he did not travel to Mexico and join in the fighting, then whatever happened to Ambrose Bierce? According to Neale, Bierce had often vowed to die by his own hand as a refusal to suffer the debilities of old age. Neale claims that Bierce had received as a present a German revolver which he "said he would use when the time should come for him to blow out his brains." He continues, "That would be the manner of his passing: a shot through the brain: that was the soldier's way, the decent method." Neale continues:

About a year before he disappeared he took a journey through the Yellowstone National Park, explored parts of the Cañon of the Colorado, and somewhere in the gorge of the Colorado selected the place of his last earthly habitat. This was in the summer of 1912. . . . He showed me a photograph of the exact location, which I think he himself had taken with a kodak, and pointed out that there he would be protected from vultures. . . .

From the time that he selected his trysting-place with Death until we last met he would, intermittently, refer to the rendezvous—not in anticipating of joy in the prospective encounter, nor yet in sorrow, but with calm indifference. It was part of an orderly process, far more to be desired than death in bed. . . . That he fulfilled his fixed purpose, I have not the least doubt.

Neale explains why Bierce may have ventured toward Mexico without actually going there. Bierce, he believes, took the Southern Pacific route to the Grand Canyon in order to avoid asthma, attacks of which had plagued him so on his last California-to-Washington trip via a northern route the "he had to interrupt his journey several times."[41]

Unless Walter Neale is lying outright, then Bierce had indeed promised suicide, had shown a photo of the spot he had chosen for the act, and had even obtained a pistol for the purpose. Those who, with Grattan, argue that Bierce would not have committed suicide,[42] have either not read his essay, "Taking Oneself Off," or have failed to observe with what conviction Bierce argues for suicide. As he says: *"Suicide is always courageous. We call it courage in a soldier merely to face death—say to lead a forlorn hope—although he has a chance of life and a certainty of 'glory.' But the suicide does more than face death; he incurs it, and with a certainty, not of glory, but of reproach. If that is not courage we must reform our vocabulary"* (italics mine).[43]

If, as the evidence indicates, Bierce planned suicide, did he also plan what Grattan disparagingly terms "a melodramatic disappearance"?[44] Bierce was certainly capable of melodrama and had more than once perpetrated a hoax. As Fatout remarks, "In the heat of attack and parry he was never quite sure where sincerity ended and hoax began. He was so fond of hoaxes that he could reel off a tall tale with a straight face."[45] As an example, when a friend had written a Poeesque poem, says Fatout, "The old trickster proposed that it be printed anonymously as an unpublished poem by Poe. Then he (Bierce) and Carrington should chip in with learned comments to prove the poem a forgery, and thus bring in enough letters to start a good argument." The hoax, however, "fizzled because Ambrose had just taken himself off the paper."[46]

So far then, we have an "old trickster" who was fond of hoaxes and who not only believed suicide was courageous but who had apparently vowed the same for himself. We know too that he was intrigued by "mysterious disappearances." In light of all this, it certainly seems plausible that Bierce planned a final hoax—the deliberately contrived, mysterious ending of his own life.

Bierce's decision to end his life rather than suffer the increasing debilities of old age probably matured in 1912 when he was seventy. He put his affairs in order with an implicit finality reminiscent of his own disappearance tales. He spoke or wrote his good-byes, then— no doubt slipping his German revolver into his pocket—set out from Washington, D.C., in October of 1913. Most likely his true destination was the Grand Canyon, about which (as early as 1910) he had written, "I'd like to lay my bones thereabout."[47] To enhance the effect of his vanishing—as he had done with some of his disappearing characters—he would want to be quite visible immediately before. So, magicianlike (dressed all in black and carrying a black cane), he staged interviews with reporters. To complete the act he needed only a distracting puff of smoke, which he conjured up in the form of a turbulent Mexico as an apparent destination. He penned final communications to further the illusion he had crossed the border, but instead the old trickster deftly slipped from sight. Perhaps—sometime before grimly cocking his revolver a few days later—he smiled wryly at the ironic thought that it was a different crossing over he was about to make.

There are some indications that this may have been, in fact, what Bierce actually did. Grenander states:

In early 1913, when he transferred a California cemetery lot to Helen, he said he did "not wish to lie there. That matter is all arranged and you will not be bothered about the mortal part of
Your Daddy."[48]

How could Bierce be certain that his "mortal part" would not be recovered, with the burden of burial expenses and arrangements not falling to his daughter? Clearly, one way would be to insure that he disappeared as utterly as the characters in his own disappearance tales. At least his giving up his cemetery plot seems to have been more than a matter of his not wishing to lie in a particular place. Perhaps he felt that while he could not escape death he could somehow cheat the grave, which he defined in his *The Devil's Dictionary* as "a place in which the dead are laid to await the coming of the medical student." A cemetery, he wrote, was "an isolated suburban spot where mourners match lies, poets write at a target, and stone-cutters spell for a wager." To Bierce, embalm meant "to cheat vegetation by locking up the gases upon which it feeds." And Edmund Wilson notes that Bierce "would not allow the graves of his children and his wife to be marked in any way."[49]

Bierce does seem to have played games with his final communications, even if we rely only on those which are accepted as genuine. We recall his postscript: "You need not believe *all* that these newspapers say of me and my purposes. I had to tell them *something*." Again, on at least one occasion after he had embarked on his final journey he sent a letter to his niece with an erroneous heading of Laredo, Texas, November 6, 1913. As he explained: "I wrote you yesterday at San Antonio, but dated the letter here and today, expecting to bring the letter and mail it here. That's because I did not know if I would have time to write it here. Unfortunately, I forgot and posted it, with other letters, where it was written. Thus does man's guile come to naught."[50]

Even if we accept Bierce's explanation of this false heading, it does alert us to the possibility that his "guile" may have extended to other letters—that he may have deliberately fabricated the sojourn into Mexico as a blind for his real purpose. Otherwise, why instruct Miss Christiansen (if indeed he did) to destroy his letters? Certainly his stated intentions to go into Mexico range from the coy (he says he has a "pretty definite purpose, which, however, is not at present disclosable"), through the vacillating ("if I can get through without being stood up against a wall and shot" and "I ought to be fairly safe if I don't have too much money on me"), to the contradictory (he does think being shot "a pretty good way to depart this life"). Perhaps he really meant it when he told Lora, "I . . . don't know where I shall be next. Guess it doesn't matter much." [51]

In any event, as apparent proof that Bierce did intend to disappear completely, there is his promise (quoted by Fatout[52]), "And nobody will find my bones." Indeed, no one has.

Following Bierce's mysterious disappearance in late 1913, the legends of his demise multiplied, as we have seen. Bierce was said to have died in battle, being alternately reported as fighting on the side of Villa's forces or on that of Carranza's. Scarcely had the journalists tamped the last spadeful of earth on Bierce's unidentified grave than they had the old soldier's body exhumed, as it were, restored to a semblance of life, and stood in front of a firing squad. Or If that were not true, then surely, they thought, Pancho Villa had ordered Bierce dispatched to his final siesta in the dark of a Mexican night. One can only imagine that it was the ghost of the selfsame Bierce who later appeared briefly with Kitchener in Europe, only to vanish yet again. As Carey McWilliams noted in 1931: "Of late the mystery surrounding the disappearance of Ambrose Bierce in 1913 has become encrusted with an outlandish accretion of fanciful stories, marvelous explanations and ingenious conjectures. The newspaper writing on the subject is already voluminous and shows no sign of abating. Once a clue is run down, however, it always turns out to be false. In fact, so many bad ones have been announced that many investigators have now wearied of the chase." [53]

In a short story entitled, "Discovery," Marian Storm offered an ingenious solution to the Bierce mystery: At the time of his disappearance, Bierce had paddled "down the Chuchilango" to some sacred caverns where—mistaken by the Indians as their long-awaited "immortal priest"—he was given refuge, surrounded by the famed "secret hoard" of treasure. Here Bierce lingered in an almost ascetic existence, chuckling at the thought of the day the Indians would discover he was not truly immortal.[54]

As recently as 1972, writer Sibley S. Morrill hypothesized that Bierce had gone to Mexico as a "secret agent." As Morrill speculates, Bierce was on an intelligence mission for the United States government, assigned to gather information on Villa's forces.[55]

One would-be investigator—noting that Miss Christiansen had lived her last years in Napa, California—conjectured that Bierce had actually ended his days there in the State Insane Asylum. Another theorist explained Bierce's disappearance as being due to supernatural forces, while yet another maintained that no such person as Ambrose Bierce had ever existed.[56]

Whatever the particular theory one subscribes to, one can only agree with Carey McWilliams, who observed "Nothing so augmented the interest in Ambrose Bierce as his disappearance. Obscurity is obscurity, but disappearance is fame."[57]

In addition to all the stories of Bierce's disappearance, his own "mysterious disappearances" tales were attracting attention. Published and republished in *The Collected Works* and in separate editions of *Can Such Things Be?*, they have been discussed by critics, noted by writers on the "paranormal" such as Frank Edwards,[58] and have even been accepted as true accounts. (J. Robert Nash so relates all three narratives, even supplying details not found in Bierce's original stories.[59])

Bierce's fascination with the disappearance theme must certainly derive from his uniquely pessimistic worldview. Many of his stories represent variations on a theme: Humans—bodies or spirits—disappear suddenly (or appear just as suddenly) with as little sense of purpose as Bierce can contrive. This lack of purpose is the very *purpose* of these stories: to embody Bierce's personal philosophy that life is essentially meaningless. As he says in "Taking Oneself Off": "But we are told with tiresome iteration that we are 'put here' for some purpose (not disclosed) and have no right to retire until 'summoned'. . . . 'Put Here.' Indeed! And by the keeper of the table! We were put here by our parents—that is all that anybody knows about it; and they had no authority and probably no intention."[60] Such, at least, is Bierce's view. And evidence suggests that, as his last act and by his own hand, he merely added to it the final punctuation.

Recommended Works

Altick, Richard D. "Hunting for Manuscripts," chapter 4 of *The Scholar Adventurers*. New York: Macmillan, 1951, 86-121. Valuable hints for tracking down correspondence, journals, and other papers.

Biography and Genealogy Master Index: A Consolidated Index to More Than 415,000 Biographical Sketches in Over 55 Current and Retrospective Biographical Dictionaries. Detroit: Gale Research, 1988. A first-look source for locating brief biographies in such reference works as *Dictionary of American Biography, Contemporary Authors*, various who's whos, etc.; should be found in any sizable library's reference section.

Bowen, Catherine Drinker. *Biography: The Craft and the Calling*. Boston: Little, Brown, 1969. A successful biographer talks about why and how she works.

Eakle, Arlene H., and Johni Cerny, eds. *Sources: A Guidebook of American Genealogy*. Salt Lake City: Ancestry, 1984. Large compendium (786 pp) of resources for genealogists and local and family historians; tells how to locate and use courthouse records, gravestones, obituaries, military files, etc.

Newspapers in Microform: United States 1948-72 Washington, D.C.: Library of Congress, 1973; supplemental edition, 1978. Invaluable guide for locating copies of old newspapers (as for biographical research): Lists dates that they commenced and (if applicable) ceased publishing, the issues (by dates) that are available on microfilm, and libraries having copies.

Winks, Robin W., ed. "Tracer of Missing Persons: Biographer and Autobiographer," in *The Historian as Detective*. New York: Harper and Row, 1969, 61-86. Presents an excerpt from *Theodore Roosevelt: An Autobiography* (1913) for comparison with a parallel one from Henry F. Pringle's *Theodore Roosevelt: A Biography* (1931).

Zinsser, William, ed. *Extraordinary Lives: The Art and Craft of American Biography*. New York: American Heritage, 1986. Six biographers discuss their work: David McCullough ("The Unexpected Harry Truman"), Richard B. Sewall ("In Search of Emily Dickinson"), Paul C. Nagel ("The Adams Women"), Ronald Steel ("Living with Walter Lippmann"), Jean Strouse ("The Real Reasons"—on J.P. Morgan), and Robert A. Caro ("Lyndon Johnson and the Roots of Power").

4

Unmasking a
Nazi Monster

Investigated with John F. Fischer

An offshoot of biographical investigation—a significant one deserving special treatment—comprises cases to which a matter of identification is central. However there are varying types of "hidden identity," varying degrees of difficulty in their exposure.

Whimsical impostures are often inadvertently exposed. For example, that of young Deborah Sampson (1760-1827) had been prompted by a desire for adventure. Masquerading as a man, as Private Robert Shurtleff, she served bravely for a year and a half in the Continental Army until being hospitalized with a fever resulted in her unmasking. Honorably discharged, she soon married, raised three children, and published a narrative of her life, *The Female Review,* in 1797.[1]

Again, magician William Ellsworth Robinson (1861-1918) had merely sought to capitalize on the popularity of a Chinese conjurer who had toured America. Adopting a similar name, "Chung Ling Soo," and donning appropriate makeup and costume, for the next eighteen years he entertained western audiences with his oriental-style wizardry. Robinson maintained his disguise even off stage and spoke to reporters only through an interpreter. His imposture was revealed after an on-stage tragedy: he was mortally wounded while performing the notorious "Bullet Catching Trick." At the hospital, doctors attempting to save his life saw that his oriental coloring did not extend below the neck or above the forearms.[2]

Such unmaskings, of course, spare the investigator—or perhaps one should say, *deprive* the investigator—of challenging work. Still, there is much of that, for many questions of identity arise as time makes erasures from our collective memory and otherwise sows confusion. Often, for example, the genealogist or local historian or antiquarian is challenged to identify a person in an old photograph correctly.

As an instance, in the course of piecing together information on a pioneer Kentuckian (a founder of the county in which I grew up) I came across a published photo of an old tintype that supposedly represented him as a young man. On reflection, however, I realized he had died—at the age of 68—a decade before tintypes were invented, a fact that disproved the identification.[3] It is now believed that that photo represents a grandson *who bore the same name.*

Another case came from an antique dealer—who had obtained a carte de visite photograph of a bearded man in death. He thought it might be of Abraham Lincoln—the photo being from about the right time period—and if so would be exceedingly valuable since Mrs. Lincoln had had most such photos destroyed.[4] I did not think the dead man much resembled the assassinated president, but the photo was made from an unusual angle which distorted the features. The photographer had stood at the foot of the bed and so looked, literally, up the man's nose. This view was unlike that of any known photograph of Lincoln.[5]

What was needed was an investigative strategy: a means of making a comparison of the features in the questioned photo with those of the sixteenth president. A statue could have been photographed from the unusual angle but would have only represented an artist's conception. Finally I recalled an actual life mask of Lincoln,[6] a copy of which was in a local museum, and I obtained permission to remove it from its display case for study. Photographer Robert H. van Outer was able to photograph it from the requisite angle and to make a print of it beside an enlargement from the questioned photo. It was then easy to see that the features were not compatible.

Yielding more positive results was a problem encountered by University of Kentucky professor of English, Joseph Gardner. A photograph had been handed down in his family, clearly labeled to indicate that it depicted the wife of a particular ancestor. The problem was that that ancestor had remarried after his first wife's death, so there were two candidates for the identification. Professor Gardner not only wished to know which wife was shown but whether she was the one from whom he had descended. The matter was resolved when he detected a slight droop in one of the woman's eyelids, an inheritable trait that was known in his own ancestry.

A far different and greater challenge, a mystery that lasted four centuries, was that of identifying the author of the celebrated *Morte D'Arthur* (1485). This collection of tales about King Arthur and his knights of the Round Table was not only among the first printed in English, but is a literary classic. Yet all that was known about its author came from a formulaic "explicit" at the end of the book: "I praye you all Ientyl men and Ientyl wymmen that redeth this book of Arthur and hys knyghtes . . . praye for me whyle I am on lyue that god sende me good delyueraunce & whan I am deed I praye you all praye for my soule for this book was ended the ix yere of the reygne of kyng edward the fourth by syr Thomas Maleore knyght as Ihesu helpe hym for hys grete myght as he is the seruaunt of Ihesu bothe day and nyght." This meant that the quarry was someone named Thomas Maleore (or Mallore, Malory, Mallery, or other phonetic variant), who had been knighted, and who was living in 1469-70 (the ninth year of Edward IV's reign).[7]

The nineteenth-century scholar George Lyman Kittredge of Harvard launched a systematic investigation of the matter, beginning by assembling the names and locales of pre-1485 Englishmen with the Malory surname. From these he discovered one who matched all the criteria: Sir Thomas Malory of Newbold Revel, Warwickshire, who had been a member of Parliament and who died on March 14, 1471.[8]

In the 1920s a former student of Kittredge's made a search of the Public Record Office in London hoping to turn up something further on Thomas Malory of Newbold Revel. He was astonished to uncover indictments for Malory on a litany of charges: extortions, rapes, robberies, an attempt (perpetrated with "26 other malefactors and breakers of the King's Peace, armed and arrayed in a warlike manner") to ambush the Duke of Buckingham, and escaping from jail. Could such a person have written the admired *Morte D'Arthur* that celebrated knightly behavior?[9]

The answer came from a rare manuscript of the *Morte D'Arthur* dating from Malory's own time. It had reposed in a library for a century before being identified in 1934. Unlike the first printed copy of the book, which had been edited, the text of the manuscript remained relatively unaltered. The text contained two additional "explicits" (rather like the one quoted earlier) which the publisher had excised. One desired "that God sende hym good delyveraunce sone and hastely" (as from jail), and the other explained, "for this was drawn by a kynght presoner sir Thomas Malleorre." This proof that the knight was also a prisoner confirmed that the celebrated author was indeed the notorious Sir Thomas Malory of Newbold Revel.[10]

From more recent history comes a case in which the subject deliberately hid his identity, not only by changing his name and using false passports but also by employing disguise.[11] Having international scope and profound implications, this was the pursuit of an embodiment of evil: Dr. Josef Mengele, whose Nazi medical "experiments" resulted in his being termed "The Angel of Death."

The case was solved only posthumously, after Mengele's identity was finally leaked by a nephew in 1985. But in the end, the real challenge of identification fell to modern forensic science. There were no fingerprints to prove that "Wolfgang Gerhard" was indeed the infamous Auschwitz physician, but there were handwriting samples, dental records, and other evidence, including the skeletal remains. An international team of experts was dispatched to the São Paulo, Brazil, police headquarters.[12]

Among the sophisticated techniques employed was that of "electronic supraposition," used to compare the questioned skull with a verified photograph of Mengele. Two video cameras were used together with a video mixer: an image of the skull was superimposed onto an actual-size copy of the photo, and points of correspondence were noted.[13]

Everything matched: the facial structure, a distinctive gap between the upper front teeth, a broken left finger, the height (174 centimeters). The handwriting in a "Gerhard" diary was also that of Mengele. Concluded authors Gerald L. Posner and John Ware in their *Mengele: The Complete Story:* "For the sake of the civilized world's peace of mind, these scientists had performed one worthwhile experiment on an unworthy life."[14]

Posner and Ware launched their own historical investigation of the case, following up the conclusive identification with an analysis of Mengele's life—from his strict Catholic upbringing, through his involvement in the death and mutilation of thousands at Auschwitz, to the more than half of his life spent as a fugitive. Their exclusive access to the Mengele papers—they sifted through more than 5,000 pages—allowed them to learn how he had been aided by a network of supporters, as well as to gain insights into the thoughts of one who had remained an unrepentant fascist.[15]

The identification of another brutal Nazi—the case of "Ivan the Terrible" which we now take up—parallels the unmasking of Mengele in many respects. But it also presents a different set of challenges and some additional lessons for the historical investigator.

During 1942-43 they arrived at Treblinka, some fifty miles east of Warsaw, in daily trainloads—Jewish families being "resettled," they were told, and taking with them such possessions as they could carry. Had they looked more closely, however, they could have seen that the "transfer station" was something quite different: only a single track ran by the platform, and the hands on the big sation house clock were merely painted on.[16]

But as they emerged from the boxcars, the Nazi SS[17] guards hurried them along, men steered one way, women and children directed another. Inside the "station" they found themselves in a barracks where they were ordered to strip naked. They were then herded into a large room with benches where their hair was shorn. (Later it would be baled and used to make felt for the war effort. Already their possessions were being sorted: fountain pens here; eyeglasses there; valuables, cash, good clothing—each in its own place, soon to be shipped to Germany. Scrapbooks and photographs were burned.)

Now they were driven outside, naked parents carrying naked children in their arms, whipped, urged at a panic-pace by rifle butts and snarling dogs down a 90-meter path the Nazis dubbed *Himmelweg*, "The road to Heaven." At the end of the path, out of sight around a bend, was their final destination: a forbidding stone structure. They were brutally driven inside by two Ukrainians: Ivan and an assistant, Nikolai.

What happened next was described by a survivor of Treblinka, writing before the end of the war: "The bedlam lasted only a short while, for soon the door[s] were slammed shut. The chamber was filled, the motor turned on and connected with the inflow pipes and, within twenty-five minutes at the most, all lay stretched out dead or, to be more accurate were standing up dead. Since there was not an inch of free space, they just leaned against each other. Even in death, mothers held their children tightly in their arms. There were no more friends or foes. There was no more jealousy. All were equal."[18]

After the mass execution, so-called "work-Jews" were forced to

drag out the bodies, remove the gold teeth, and push the wagon-
loaded corpses to the pits. Originally they were simply dumped
and covered with lime and sand, but a more efficient disposal
system was needed. Therefore, a "grill" was fashioned from railroad tracks and the bodies were burned, producing a perpetual
haze over the Polish landscape.

Ivan—who had actually volunteered for the gruesome work in
order to get out of POW camp—served at Treblinka for more than a
year, during which perhaps as many as a million Jews were executed in this cowardly fashion. Ivan served as a mechanic, main-
taining and repairing the motor that pumped the carbon monoxide
into the death chambers.

According to contemporary descriptions—including one taken
from a camp-survivor's diary of 1945—Ivan was about twenty-five
years old, was tall and muscular, and had eyes that "seemed kind
and gentle."[19] However, he was a sadist, known to hack off an ear
or split skulls with a gas pipe he brandished. Since the work-Jews
did not know his last name, they called him *Ivan Grozny* (after a
former Russian czar who had himself killed countless Jews): "Ivan
the Terrible."

Over the next three decades Ivan's whereabouts were unknown. But in 1975 the name of a man living in Cleveland appeared
on a list of suspected Ukrainian war criminals supplied by an
informant (a Ukrainian living in the United States). Two years later
the Immigration and Naturalization Service included the man's
picture in a photospread (or "photo lineup") sent to Israel in the
case of Feodor Fedorenko, a former guard at the Polish death camp.
At the time, the Cleveland man was not even suspected of having
been at Treblinka, his photo merely being included as one of seven
extras to complete the lineup.

Nevertheless, in Israel, Elijahu Rosenberg, who had escaped
from Treblinka in a 1943 uprising, carefully studied the photospread
while an investigator from the Nazi War Crimes Unit of the Israel
National Policy waited patiently. Soon Rosenberg identified
Fedorenko. Then he pointed to another photo: this was Ivan from
Treblinka, he said.[20]

The photograph was that of the suspected war criminal from
Cleveland. It was taken from the 1951 visa application of John Demjanjuk. Two other Treblinka survivors were summoned to Israeli
police headquarters to study the photospread. Independently, each

looked at the eight pictures, then pointed to the one Rosenberg had selected. Each identified it as that of Ivan from Treblinka.

As it turned out, Demjanjuk (pronounced "dem-yan-yook") had anglicized his first name from *Ivan*. He had been born Ivan Demjanjuk at Dub Macharenzi in the Ukraine in 1920. A big, beefy fellow, he matched the description of Ivan from Treblinka. And, curiously, as if he had simply resumed his former livelihood, he was *working as a motor mechanic* at the Ford Motor Company plant in Cleveland.

Moreover, he had lied about his background when he immigrated to America, covering up his Russian military service and subsequent capture by the Germans with the claim that he had been a farmer in Sobibor, Poland, during the war. Actually, there was another death camp at Sobibor, and there is evidence that Demjanjuk was there as well.

In 1981 Demjanjuk was given a chance to explain his reason for lying. The opportunity arose when the United States Department of Justice prosecuted him in federal court in Cleveland, seeking to revoke his American citizenship. Testifying in Ukrainian, through an interpreter, Demjanjuk said he had been motivated by fear of repatriation: "Because I had been a soldier of the Red Army and there was a regulation that if you were going to be taken prisoner of war, you had to shoot yourself, and I hadn't done so."[21]

The prosecution, however, attempted to show through the testimony of various federal officials that by 1951, when his visa had been granted, Demjanjuk had little cause to fear repatriation. In fact, Demjanjuk admitted that his "strongest fear" had been during 1945-47. On the other hand, he would have had an obvious motive for lying if he had been on the staff of a Nazi death camp: No such person would have been eligible to receive a displaced-person visa for admittance to the United States. Indeed, defection to the Nazis could have provided a real reason to fear repatriation.

Demjanjuk fared even worse when he attempted to account for his whereabouts during the war, especially the critical period between the summer of 1942 and the fall of 1943, the time "Ivan the Terrible" was exterminating Jews. Under sustained cross-examination, Demjanjuk was often reduced to saying, "I don't know," or "I can't say exactly."[22] He committed a serious blunder when he repeatedly maintained he had been a prisoner at the POW camp at Chelm, Poland, until October 1944. Actually the camp had been abandoned ten months before, as an expert established, thus discrediting Demjanjuk's alibi.

More than six years later—after he had been stripped of his American citizenship, deported to Israel, and placed on trial for war crimes and crimes against humanity—Demjanjuk was still blaming a faulty memory, together with his fourth-grade education, for what the Associated Press termed "contradictions in his testimony about his whereabouts during the war." In the course of weeklong cross-examination, he said, "My tragic mistake is I can't think properly. I don't know how to answer."[23]

The most incriminating evidence against Ivan/John Demjanjuk—presented at both trials—was an SS identification card, bearing what appeared to be his photograph and signature. (See Figure 6.) It surfaced as a result of the efforts of Allan A. Ryan, Jr., who became a "Nazi hunter" in 1979 when he took command of the U.S. Department of Justice's newly created Office of Special Investigations (OSI). When Ryan inherited the previous INS file on Demjanjuk, and thus discovered that three Treblinka survivors had identified Demjanjuk from a photospread, he cabled Moscow. Ryan knew that in 1944 the Soviets had captured the SS facility, Trawniki, where death-camp guards had been trained, and he thought the Soviets might have retained the captured records.

In January of 1980 OSI received from the Soviet archives a photocopy of the incriminating Trawniki ID card. Together with the name Ivan Demjanjuk was the information that he was born on April 3, 1920, that his father's name was Nikolai, that he had a scar on his back. All were true for John Demjanjuk, as he admitted in U.S. federal court, but he was evasive. Was it his signature? "I don't think so." His photograph? "I cannot say. Possibly it is me."

Because the eyewitness Rosenberg (who had been first to pick him out of the photospread in Israel) had testified that Ivan's eyes had been gray, Demjanjuk's attorney queried his client: "What color are your eyes?" "Blue." "What color were your eyes in 1942?" "Blue." However, a prosecuting attorney returned to the issue on cross-examination:

"This card indicates that the Ivan Demjanjuk [described thereon] has gray eyes. You indicated to your attorney that you have always had blue eyes, is that correct?"
"Yes."

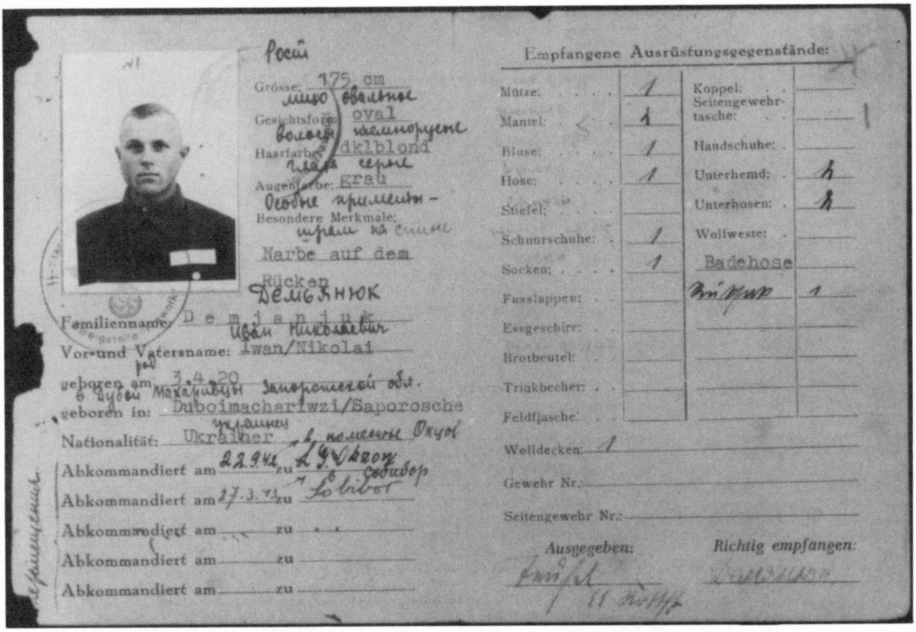

Figure 6. Nazi SS training camp ID card in the name of Ivan Demjanjuk bears his photograph. Eyewitnesses have identfied him as "Ivan the Terrible," the sadistic guard who previously operated the gas-chamber motor at Treblinka where up to a million Jews were executed. Although the card indicates Demjanjuk was posted to two other places, including the death camp at Sobibor, according to Israeli authorities he was also dispatched at times to Treblinka.

"Do you see the color of the eyes in this visa application?" (He handed Demjanjuk the application bearing his signature.)

"I don't see it."

"Let me help you." (He pointed to the place.) "Would you tell us the color of the eyes in this visa application?"

"Gray."[24]

It was the question of the ID card's authenticity that most intrigued John Fischer and me when we were asked to become involved in the case. (John is an outstanding forensic analyst in a Florida crime laboratory who has worked with me for more than a decade on cases ranging from homicide investigation to uncovering bogus "spirit pictures."[25])

In mid-August of 1987 an agent for the family called from Toronto to ask if we would be willing to receive a packet of materials relating to the prosecution of Demjanjuk, and to suggest the possi-

Figure 7. Photograph from Nazi SS identification card (left) has been identified by death-camp survivors as that of "Ivan the Terrible." A few years later the face has become less muscular and the hairline is receding a bit, as shown by the photo from a 1947 driver's license (right) issued to Ivan (now John) Demjanjuk.

bility of our writing an investigative article. We agreed, and were subsequently put in touch with Demjanjuk's son-in-law, Edward Nishnic, the president of the John Demjanjuk Defense Fund. After acquainting ourselves with the basic facts in the case, we opened our review-investigation.

We focused on the Nazi identification card, a five-by-seven-inch document folded in half. Clearly, it it were authentic it would mean that during the time of the atrocities at Treblinka Ivan/John Demjanjuk was not farming in Poland (as he had lied to American immigration officials) nor confined in concentration camps (as he later maintained, albeit with contradictions). (The concurrent claim— that he had served in 1944 with a so-called "Russian Army of Liberation" unit established by the Germans—was essentially irrelevant, doing little more than prove that Demjanjuk had been, in fact, a member of at least one Nazi unit.)[26] The ID card would actually place him at Trawniki, a former sugar factory the SS had transformed into a training compound for death-camp guards.[27] This would be damning indeed.

On the other hand, Demjanjuk's defenders, notably conserva-

Figure 8. Photograph of John Demjanjuk from his 1958 naturalization certificate (left) is compared with the photo from the SS identification card by overlaying transparencies (right). Note the strong resemblance to the interim (1947) photograph from the driver's license (figure 7). (Photo by John F. Fischer.)

tive columnist Patrick J. Buchanan, have suggested the card was the product of a Soviet "KGB forgery factory." It was supposedly made to order to fulfill the American request for information about Demjanjuk. But why would the Soviets wish to frame an innocent U.S. autoworker who, Buchanan admits, "was neither an outspoken anti-communist, nor a leader in the American-Ukrainian community?" Buchanan concedes this is an "excellent question."[28]

The consensus among Demjanjuk defenders seems to be the notion advanced during his Jerusalem trial. As *Time* reported, "The defense contends that the card is a forgery by the Soviet KGB as part of an effort to harass the Ukrainian community in the U.S."[29] Another suggestion was that the card was forged so that "at a later date" the Soviets could "seriously embarrass Israel"[30] (as if they would not seriously embarrass themselves in the process).

We began our study of the matter with the photograph on the ID card, to determine whether it was indeed that of the accused war criminal. We had available to us color enlargements of the front and back of the card plus a much greater black-and-white blowup of the photo it bore. For comparison, we had obtained authenticated photographs of the accused, notably, from his 1947 German driver's license (see Figure 7), another from his 1958 naturalization certificate, plus other related materials including a videotape produced for the Israeli prosecution.

In addition to our own analyses—which included a close comparison by one of us (who had a background in portraiture), an overlay of photo-transparencies by the other (a forensic analyst),[31] and other studies (see Figure 8)—we submitted the photographs to five specialists. Each had backgrounds in some aspect of facial identification.

The first two—a police commander, Lt. Drexel T. Neal, and a detective, Sgt. Raleigh S. Pate,[32]—were experienced in "Identikit" facial-feature comparisons, police lineups, and the like. Each expressed the strong opinion that the photos represented the same individual, citing various details of the features (nostrils, ears, hairline, etc.) in support.

Our third specialist was Glenn Taylor, a professional portrait artist of many years' experience who has assisted us in several important cases. His feature-by-feature comparison was quite detailed, calling attention to such factors as "pronounced central nasal-laboid groove," "degree of lip eversion," and the like, as well as the "general relationship of features to each other," all of which, he concluded, indicated the photos depicted "the same man at three different ages." Taylor noted that "the greater mass of the jaw musculature shown in the earlier photo" (that of the ID card) was probably "attributable to the pronounced muscle tone of a youthful and active man."[33] (Recall that the Nazi, Ivan, at Treblinka, had been described in a survivor's diary as particularly "muscular."[34])

The fourth expert, Dr. Virginia Smith, is an anthropologist with expertise in reconstructing faces from human skulls. She stated:

The soft tissue configuration of the face and ears, and the progressive pattern baldness lead me to conclude that the three photographs represent the same individual. This opinion, however, is made without the more conclusive comparison of the hard tissue.

The faces represented in these photographs could conform to a single skull structure. This structure is characterized by heavy brow development that is aligned in the same manner with the nasal bones in all of the photographs. All photographs show broad zygomatic arches, and a slightly higher right orbital arch. The right orbit is also slightly larger in all photographs.[35]

We regarded this determination of distinctively similar bone structure exhibited in the questioned and known photographs as particularly telling.

Finally, because of the high identification value of the human ear, the configurations of which are quite distinctive (albeit less so than fingerprint patterns), we contacted an internationally known expert in the field. Alfred V. Iannarelli has been consulted in such celebrated identification cases as those of Martin Borman, Anastasia, Lindbergh, the two "Will Wests," and many others, including the case of Lee Harvey Oswald's imagined "double." Developer of the system of identification bearing his name, Iannarelli stated, "in reference to the Demjanjuk case of identity, I have thoroughly examined all the photographs and transparencies utilizing my system of ear identification and have come to the conclusion that the ears on these photographs are all of the same individual. In addition, it is my opinion that the photograph on the identification card *is not* a Soviet forgery, but indeed, that of Mr. Demjanjuk." He added:

My congratulations to the photographer who made the photographic enlargements of Demjanjuk; the contrast and details were excellent. Each photo clearly illustrates the anatomical structure of the subject's left ear permitting me to make the comparison and identification *without any hesitation or doubt*. The protrusion of Demjanjuk's left ear in all the photographs was sufficiently pronounced and producing details of each ear image with sufficient contrast that it was not necessary to use the method I used in the Lindbergh identity case such as the Computer Image Enhancement process or the Sobel Edge Detection technique (Emphasis added).[36]

We concurred with all five opinions.

Because Iannarelli is also an expert in identification photographs, we then asked him to review an analysis of the photos that had been done for the Israeli prosecution, and to comment on the possibility of their having been retouched. He subsequently replied, "I could not detect any evidence of photographic retouching," and again, "I could find no evidence of tampering with the ID photograph either with the facial features or the clothing."[37]

The issue of retouching has become important since an expert in document examination, William Flynn, has stated that "the 'Demjanjuk photograph' on the ID card contains the same featureless, white background as typically results from airbrushing." Of course, in what is probably a ratio of millions to one, so do countless genuine photographs. But Mr. Flynn also calls attention to a misalignment of the photo with the rubber-stamp seals that overlap onto it, as well as evidence that the photo had twice been glued to the card, and that a set of staple holes indicate (since there are no corresponding holes in the card itself) that the photo was once attached to another document.[38]

Mr. Flynn seems unaware, however, that instead of having a plausible theory he has pieces of two very different scenarios. He hypothesizes that a genuine face of Demjanjuk could have been superimposed onto the face of a man in a German uniform,[39] but such work would have required rephotographing a doctored original, or creating a new print from altered negatives. Either way, the resulting new photograph would have no staple holes. Moreover, the famous McCrone Associates laboratory found that the photographic paper was consistent with archival samples of 1941-43 supplied by a German photographic firm. Actually the most likely explanation for the staple holes is that the photograph had been temporarily affixed to an *application* for the identification card—a common practice with many passport and other photos.[40]

As to the misalignment and regluing, their cause is quite apparent. The similar Trawniki cards available for comparison had loose or even missing photos, with old smears of glue where they had fallen off. Gideon Epstein, senior forensic document analyst, United States Department of the Treasury, testified that when he examined the card in 1981 (the time of Demjanjuk's first trial), "the photograph was loose enough to move with your hand, so that you could get some sort of play into the photograph. And . . . with this type of movement I was able to correctly align the seal so that there was exact alignment. In my 1987 examination . . . I found that the photograph was very firmly affixed so that it could not be moved.[41] In other words, between the two trials someone—likely the card's Soviet custodian—had reglued the loose photo to prevent its dropping off as others had.

We now turned to the larger question of forgery. After all, while we determined the photograph was an authentic one, positively that of Ivan/John Demjanjuk, naturally that did not preclude its having been affixed to a forged ID card. And Demjanjuk's defenders had raised numerous points that they felt indicated the card must be fraudulent.

For example there was the matter of the reported death of "Ivan the Terrible," killed—according to some sources—in a Jewish uprising at Treblinka in August 1943. In fact, no one really knew what had happened to "Ivan,"[42] who may well have been injured in the fighting. Reports of his death, to borrow from Mark Twain, may have been greatly exaggerated.

But much of the focus was on the damning card itself. There were early attempts to discredit it on the basis of perceived errors in wording, such as the use of the feminine *Bluse* ("blouse") for the masculine *Hemd* ("shirt"); and there were questions of typography, e.g., a missing umlaut over a *u*.[43] We learned, however, that *Bluse* was actually correct in German military usage for "field jacket,"[44] and the other details are probably the result of the cards' having been *printed in Poland* by a consequently non-German printer lacking a German type font.

Other "evidence" cited by the defense was reminiscent of that in the ludicrous case of Oswald's "double": Demjanjuk's height given on the identification card was in error.[45] But as the Oswald case actually demonstrated, some people don't know their correct measurement, or may misstate it, or lie out of vanity. Still others may have their height filled in for them by a harried clerk looking up from a typewriter. Why would clever KGB forgers not be able to obtain Demjanjuk's correct height from his Soviet Red Army papers, if they were thorough enough to learn of a scar on his back?

Defense attorneys at the sensational trial in Jerusalem carefully cross-examined the prosecution's expert document examiners— Epstein,[46] Amnon Bezalely (an Israeli Police examiner with expertise in handwriting, typewriting, printing, etc.),[47] and Dr. Antonio Cantu (document examiner with the U.S. Treasury Department and a distinguished expert in the forensic examination of inks, paper, and the like).[48]

Stated very briefly, the experts' findings were that the card was of cheap paper stock consistent with its purported time of issuance (and free of various synthetic fibers, optical brighteners, and resins introduced into paper after the early 1940s); that its letterpress printing and photograph were likewise consistent; that its typewritten portions were produced on a 1930-series "Olympia 12" machine; that the ink for the portions of rubber-stamp impressions that were on the photograph matched those that extended onto the card; and that all of the various inks on the card had analytical (e.g., thin-layer-chromatographic) profiles similar to those available in 1942, and none had characteristics of inks manufactured after that time.[49]

The handwriting experts were well aware of the possibility of error in such a case as this. Amnon Bezalely actually had experience in detecting Soviet forgeries,[50] and Gideon Epstein had written about the Frank Walus case which had resulted in the persecution of an innocent man as an alleged Nazi war criminal. Stated Epsetin, "The Walus case, more than anything else, clearly demonstrates the importance of documentary evidence as opposed to eye-witnesses."[51]

Nevertheless, the experts determined that the surname-only signatures of Ernst Teufel (the camp quartermaster) and Kurt Streibel (Trawniki commandant) were undoubtedly authentic. They based their conclusions on comparisons, including stereo-microscopic examination, with known exemplars obtained from German archives. As Gideon Epstein stated,

In light of the various examinations that I conducted of the document, at the Soviet Embassy, on February 27th 1981, and later of the signatures and the comparison of that writing and the identification of the individuals Streibel and Teufel as making those signatures, my conclusion to the overall document is that it is a genuine document, that it does not bear any evidence of being authored, text substituted, or in any way fraudulently prepared. And as a result I feel that the document is what it purports to be, what it purports to represent and is therefore genuine.[52]

There were various problems inhibiting authentication of the surname signature "Demjanjuk," including the fact it was penned in Ukrainian (Cyrillic) characters, that the comparison signatures dated from several years later, that many of them were in Latin characters written in ballpoint, and so forth. Nevertheless Bezalely concluded that it lacked the conspicuous indications of forgery and appeared to be "an authentic signature as far as the pace in which it was written is concerned."[53]

We very carefully and critically reviewed all of these findings. Additionally, we made our own assessment of the "Teufel" and "Streibel" autographs by comparing color-photo enlargements of them with reproduction-enlargements of those men's signatures. Early on, one retouched stroke of the latter came in for particular scrutiny, but we determined it lacked the pattern of frequent and careful retouchings that can point toward forgery and was instead the type of single, bold retouching that is often characteristic of a genuine signature.[54] We later learned that microscopic inspection revealed the absence of any attendant, suspicious pen-lifts, and that the coarse paper had apparently caused the pen to skip, necessitating the quickly jotted retouch.[55]

As to the "Demjanjuk" signature, we considered the fact of his near-illiteracy (fourth-grade education) in 1942 and the subsequent effects of modern Western culture with its demands for frequent name-signing. Whereas William Flynn has insisted that the signature contains features notably unlike those of Demjanjuk's—"a classic swirling, Slavic 'D'" and all of the letters connected[56]—shouldn't he instead be asking obvious questions? For example, why would sophisticated Soviet forgers, who supposedly had unlimited access to documents (from which to unstaple an incriminating photograph), not copy the *most obvious* features of his signature correctly?

Flynn has concocted a clever scenario. He claims "the only part of the ID card that needed to be forged was the Demjanjuk signature" since the Soviets could have captured a number of blank ID forms which they could then fill out at will to incriminate innocent folks.[57] Well, not actually blank: the cards would have had to have been *presigned* by Teufel and Streibel.

Ivan/John Demjanjuk—convicted by a judicial panel and sentenced to death in Israel—would not openly confess to the heinous crimes with which he was charged. (Never mind a televised report that he had already tacitly done so: Supposedly overheard by an Israeli marshal, Demjanjuk was quoted as saying that people did not understand, that he had to do what he did because "It was war."[58])

The question for us who wish to know the truth in the matter must therefore become one of our basic approach to the evidence: Do we start with the answer—as his defenders do—that he is innocent, and then work backward to the evidence, concocting one explanation for the eyewitnesses (they are mistaken), another for the incriminating document (it was forged), still another for Demjanjuk's having lied to U.S. Immigration officials (he was afraid of repatriation), yet another for his contradictory alibi (his memory was faulty), and so on? Such separate rationalizations do not convince.

Or do we rather look at the evidence, without preconception, no more desirous of convicting an innocent man than of setting a mass-murderer free? If so, we are led, from an almost accidental identification in Israel, to supportive identifications of a man who was indeed named Ivan, who matched contemporary descriptions, who was working at Ivan's trade of motor mechanic, who had lied about his true whereabouts during the war, who could only manage a blundering and contradictory alibi, who even admitted to serving in a Nazi-sponsored unit, and who would turn out to be the subject of an SS identification document, authenticated by sophisticated analyses and the testimony of distinguished experts.

Thus we see that the details of evidence are corroborative, that they point clearly to the guilt of John Demjanjuk. At long last, his hidden identity—as "Ivan the Terrible," mechanic of death—has been uncovered.

Recommended Works

Nickell, Joe, "Double Trouble: Synchronicity and the two Will Wests," chap. 6 of Joe Nickell (with John F. Fischer), *Secrets of the Supernatural*. Bufalo: Prometheus, 1988). Relates the case of Will and William West, criminal look-alikes whose uncanny resemblance helped advance fingerprinting in America, yet who were supposedly unrelated; investigation (including amassing documentary evidence, comparing ear patterns and inheritable traits in fingerprints, etc.) demonstrated instead that they were identical twins.

O'Hara, Charles E. *Fundamentals of Criminal Investigation*, third edition. Springfield, Illinois: Charles C. Thomas, 1973. Good introduction to police investigative procedures and basics of forensic identification.

Wyatt, Will. *The Secret of the Sierra Madre: The Man Who Was B. Traven*. San Diego: Harcourt Brace Jovanovich, 1985. Fascinating example of modern historical detective work; Wyatt succeeds in uncovering the true identity of "the *Marie Celeste* of literature," the enigmatic, reclusive author "B. Traven ": a one-time German revolutionary born Otto Feige in Schwiebus (now Poland).

Swift's Lost
Silver Mine

Although it is true that "The historian tends to think mainly in terms of documents,"[1] it is also true that he or she must frequently rely on other sources, so-called oral history being one important example. Oral history is information based on interviews with persons who have direct knowledge of historical events, as when Greek historians Thucydides and Herodotus, in the fifth century B.C., interviewed the survivors of wars they were chronicling.[2] As oral-history expert Willa K. Baum puts it, "The way of life that was characteristic of an earlier America is rapidly disappearing, but there are persons still alive today who remember it vividly. It is unlikely that they will preserve their pioneer memories by writing memoirs, as historians would wish them to do, but many old-timers are willing to tell their stories and confide their reminiscences to tape recordings. . . . While the individual recordings are sometimes fragmentary and highly personal, taken together they provide a fund of color, detail, and incident invaluable for future historical research."[3]

However, when a person is no longer imparting first-hand information, but is instead passing on that which has been handed down by oral tradition, he or she is relating "folklore" (a term coined in 1846 and variously defined).[4] Because of the limitations of folklore (for example a tale can become garbled, exaggerated, or attached to a wrong person or place[5]), the historian must handle such material judiciously.[6]

Two sets of popular American narratives help illustrate the concerns. Behind the published stories of "Johnny Appleseed," a kindly hermit who wore a tin pot on his head and wandered the countryside planting apple seedlings, lies a lively oral tradition.

And that, however exaggerated and transformed, was an out-growth of the life of the very real frontier orchardist, John Chapman (1774-1845).[7]

The stories of another mythical Yankee hero, a giant lumberjack named Paul Bunyan, are, however, quite different. The basis of tradition underlying them is really very thin, and, so far as is known, they have no real-life model. Most, in fact, are literary productions. Some were written by a newspaperman in 1910,[8] but the main source for the yarns—about Bunyan, members of his crew such as Johnny Inkslinger and Sourdough Sam, and Babe, his Blue Ox—were the later contrivances of one W.B. Laughead, advertising executive for the Red River Lumber Company of Minneapolis.

In 1949 Richard M. Dorson coined the term "fakelore" to de-scribe such manufactured folktales,[9] as well as such other pseudo-folk productions as the stylized costumes common to certain "pioneer" celebrations[10]. According to him, fakelore is a falsifica-tion of folkloric data by means of "invention, selection, fabrication, and similar refining processes."[11]

Fact, folklore, and fiction may all be interwoven into a particular legend, as witness the narratives about Jesse James. Earning a deserved reputation for outlawry, James (1847-1882) and his older brother Frank led their gang through a string of successful bank holdups until a new member, Bob Ford, slew Jesse at the behest of the Missouri governor.

Many tales about the outlaw and his band follow well-known folkloric patterns. Such is the story (in the tradition of the Returning Hero) that it was not Jesse but another who was actually killed. (Several old men have even claimed to be the "real" Jesse,[12] but with little success.)[13] Many other narratives are simply literary fictions, disseminated by hundreds of dime novels and numerous Hollywood movies.[14]

Some of the world's great legends provide instructive examples of the relationship, if any, between such narratives and actual events. For example, the biblical story of Noah's ark strikingly parallels an earlier Babylonian myth, the Gilgamesh Epic, from which it is thought to derive.[15] Yet geologists dismiss the possibility of a worldwide inundation,[16] and skeptical investigtors have of-fered numerous arguments against any true basis for the myth.[17]

In contrast is the legend of Atlantis. Putting aside the more absurd theories,[18] some scholars have suggested the legend might have derived from the ancient Minoan civilization of Crete which was largely destroyed by a volcano in the 1400s B.C. [19]

In order for historical investigators to determine the degree of credibility due a particular narrative, it must be analyzed according to appropriate criteria. [20] Corroborative evidence may also be found. Thus what Dorson calls "the presumption of historical trust-worthiness" can be increased. [21]

Dorson posits "capitalistic gain" as the impetus for fakelore. [22] But putting aside the question of motive (not always easy to determine in any case), how do we describe a case in which the source for a lengthy legendary tradition appears to have been a deliberate hoax? Or could it be that there really are historical facts and people behind the fabulous treasure tale we now examine?

For two centuries a legend has persisted in eastern Kentucky concerning the "lost silver mines" of one "Jonathan Swift." In his alleged *Journal,* Swift relates how he and a company of men preceded Daniel Boone into Kentucky, making annual trips from Alexandria, Virginia, to mine silver. From June 21, 1760, until late 1769, they "carried in supplies and took out silver bars and minted coins" which Swift used to buy vessels for his "shipping interests." Plagued by Indians, a mutiny of his workmen, and other troubles, and after a pious change of heart, Swift discontinued his venture, walled up his mine and a caveful of treasure, and headed for "England or France" to "get a party interested in. . .working the mines on a large scale." When he returned after a fifteen-year delay (he says he was imprisoned in England), Swift had become blind and unable to find his fabulous treasure. [23]

Many have undoubtedly accepted the legend at face value. As J.H. Kidwell says, "Men, hoary with age and gray haired, half insane on the subject of the Swift mines ranged the mountains and the likely places, and died in the belief that they were very near the source of the mines as outlined in the Swift *Journal.*" [24] To some a treasury warrant of 1788, whereby John Filson (the early Kentucky mapmaker and historian) recorded 1,000 acres alleged to contain Swift's mine, has lent credence to the legend. [25]

Skeptical geologists and historians have advanced quite another theory that has also achieved legendary status. [26] This theory supposes that Swift concocted the tale of silver mining as a cover for piracy and counterfeiting. Although the theory has persuaded many, it raises more questions than it answers: Why make the arduous and extremely dangerous journey to Kentucky in order to melt silver when the backwoods near Alexandria would do?[27] For that matter, the coinage could have been minted on board ship. And why go to all the trouble of producing a spurious journal? Such literary ability, employing phrases like "deeming it imprudent," is indeed remarkable for one who went to sea "when a boy."

Moreover, the scientific evidence seems to preclude fabulous silver treasure being mined in Kentucky. Warren H. Anderson of the Kentucky Geological Survey responded to my query: "From a geologic standpoint it is possible for silver to occur in sandstones in eastern Kentucky, but this does not mean that silver actually exists in economic quantities. Some silver has been reported in the western Kentucky fluorspar district . . . as well as trace amounts in the central Kentucky mineral district. . . . As these reports indicate silver does occur in small amounts in Kentucky."[28] Note that the precious metal exists only in trace amounts and in parts of Kentucky beyond the eastern section.

How this contrasts with Swift's purported find. He states he had two "workings," and that Frenchmen who "worked mines to the south" had no fewer than two furnaces in operation.[29] Swift claims he found several "veins" of silver! Such abundance—when two hundred years of highway construction, excavation, and strip mining, not to mention cave exploration and treasure hunting, have failed to unearth even a single "vein" of silver! Yet Swift alleges a wounded *bear* had led to the discovery of a cave containing "a very rich vein of silver ore."

In researching the Swift story—and doing a little prospecting myself (see Figure 9)—I came across reports of "silver nuggets" from the Wolfe County area. My cousin, John May, was able to coax one sample from its owner and gave it to me to test. It was pyrite—"fool's gold." Or in this case, fool's silver. Similarly, a U.S. Forest Service official told me he had tested samples of ore brought in to a Wolfe County ranger station and found them to be "iron sulfides," that is, pyrite. He stated he also had found samples of lead sulfide (galena), which the layperson could easily mistake for silver.

A parks official confided that about two or three years ago an attempt was made to sell the Commonwealth of Kentucky a tract of land, alleged to contain Swift's mine, for approximately a million

Figure 9. The author prospecting in a rock shelter in the Red River Gorge area of eastern Kentucky. (Photo by John May.)

dollars! Another official, he said, agreed to be taken, blindfolded, to a prospector's pit. The "silver" actually glittered: It was mica!

Clearly the geologic evidence demands that we closely scrutinize the Swift *Journal*, or rather, journals, since numerous versions compete in the claim for authenticity.[30] These differ in varying degrees. One, headed "John Swift's Manuscript Journal," begins, "I was born October 3, 1712, in Philadelphia, Pennsylvania, my ancestors first came to America in 1637."[31] Another, from Tennessee, commences; "I, George William Swift, was born at Salisbury, England in the year of 1689, A.D., a son of William Swift, who was a miner of copper, silver, and lead."[32] Even versions with some distinct similarities contain discrepancies in dates and number of the excursions as well as the directions for finding the mines.

Probably the most detailed version is reproduced in Michael Paul Henson's *John Swift's Lost Silver Mines*.[33] But it demands skepticism: A journal which begins, "I was born . . ." is immediately suspect. This version does agree substantially with quoted fragments from *History of Kentucky*.[34] But portions of the history-book text, wherein Swift is alternately paraphrased and quoted, seem to have been "lifted" by the unknown compiler of this particular version of the *Journal*.

Some of the *paraphrased* portions are recorded word for word in the *Journal*. Further, the latter work carelessly preserves one quoted excerpt *in quotation marks* with the untenable result of having Swift begin quoting himself in mid-sentence![35] Another discrepancy involves the ending of the *Journal*, allegedly penned by Swift after his return from England, although in it he states that he has become completely blind and therefore would have been unable to write![36]

And what of the statement, "that treasure will lie in that cave for eternity," written (if the *Journal* can be believed) during 1765?[37] Why would Swift pen such a hopelessly defeatist remark, one anticipating events not to be realized for twenty years, while he was still making excursions to the mines?

Was there really a John or Jonathan Swift? Well, of course, there was the famous English satirist by that name who wrote the allegorical *Travels Into Several Remote Nations of the World* (better known as *Gulliver's Travels*). Like "Swift," "Gulliver" was a ship's captain and the title of "his" work is echoed in a phrase from Swift's *Journal* stating that the smelting furnace was "in a very remote place in the west."[38] But that Jonathan Swift died in 1745. It would seem that, at best, he could have only have unwittingly inspired the creation of a Swift legend.

At the end of the *Journal* in Henson's book is added a "cut signature" (as collectors of autograph materials say) of "Jonathan Swift." Henson says he placed it there "to lend a touch of authenticity to the document. This is an exact reproduction of Swift's signature that appears on an old land grant I obtained from an attorney in Kentucky."[39] But Mr. Henson is in error.

I researched the matter, finally tracking down the entire deed from which the actual signature in question was reproduced.[40] I carefully compared the signatures and found them to be identical, stroke for stroke. The document does substantiate that there really was a bona-fide Jonathan Swift and that he was from Alexandria, Virginia, as the *Journal* alleges, and further that he was a "merchant" (which at that port, could mean that he had shipping interests as claimed).

Unfortunately, further research proved Mr. Swift reacquired the land and deeded it a second time in 1809[41]—nine years after "Swift's" reputed death."[42] The documents also enabled me to establish that the "signature" on the first deed was not actually by Swift's own hand but was, like the entire document, in the hand-writing of the recorder who had copied it into the deed book!

This real Mr. Jonathan Swift could not have been the Swift of silver-mine mythology, as will be clear from his biography. It informs us that he "was born at Milton, near Boston, Mass., and became a resident of Alexandria prior to 1785; was an importing merchant and prominent citizen during the forty years of his residence." He married and had "several children." He died in 1824 and "was buried with Masonic honors."[43] Clearly Mr. Swift was not the supposed blind pirate, nor is it likely he reached the remarkable age of one hundred and twelve years!

The genealogical data of some versions of the *Journal* must be discounted. Not journals—but brazen attempts to perpetrate fraud—begin so. (Some details even appear to have been copied, usually carelessly and quite late, from Swift genealogies.[44]) Indeed the *earliest references* to the legend mention only "a Certain man named Swift,"[45] "one Swift,"[46] "Swift,"[47] and "said Swift."[48] (And the Tennessee version cited previously gives an entirely different first name.) There *were* numerous Swifts. Some were actually named John or Jonathan, which is, after all, a common first name. But there is *no proof* that there was an actual person named "Swift," whether "Jonathan" or not, who early mined silver in Kentucky.

We turn now to the seemingly exact directions for locating the mines which make up the latter part of the *Journal* and which have inspired thousands of searches. But just how exact are they? We can take a cue from the coy statement therein that the furnace is "in a very remote place in the west." Landmarks are liberally given together with some directions and distances. Naturally these vary from version to version.

Although Swift maps have been widely reputed to exist, they are scarce in relation to copies of the *Journal*.[49] So, with the help of my father—who often acted as a guide in the Red River area, and who read maps at his leisure—I constructed a hypothetical map of the mines and buried treasure. I based it primarily on the rather detailed version of the *Journal* in Henson's book (see Figure 10). It was immediately apparent that great flexibility of interpretation was required, pointing up the true vagueness of the description.

But Swift actually gives the latitude and longitude of the mines: "The richest ore is to be found in Latitude of 37° 56 minutes north

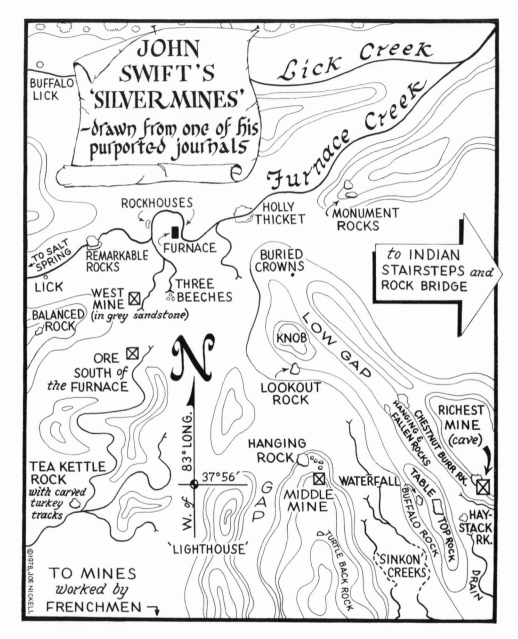

Figure 10. Map reconstructed from purported journal description shows supposed location of John Swift's lost silver mines. (Drawing by author.)

[some versions read "57 minutes"]. The ore vein of little value is in Latitude of 38° 2 minutes north. By astronomical observations and calculations, we found both veins to be just a little west of the longitude of 83 degrees."[50] While this is seemingly specific, exactly how far is "just a little" west?

Taken literally, the latitude and longitude of "the richest ore" pinpoint a location in Morgan County (from which I am writing) near Relief, Kentucky. Alas, neither the proper configuration nor the mine is to be found there. Despite all this, several factors conspire to fuel the search: Errors in "Swift's" calculations are reasonably assumed; partial configurations are locations or "interpreted" as necessary; new maps and alleged copies of the *Journal* are drafted; newspaper editors experience weeks in which no man bites a dog; and skeptics are shunned by a public eager to believe.

And so virtually every county in eastern Kentucky lays claim to the silver mines. As well, the legend persists in Virginia, West Virginia, Tennessee, and North Carolina; and presumably it is everywhere good for business. A "Monument Rock" here, a "Balanced Rock" there, is often enough to set metal detectors and spades—even heavy equipment—in motion.

At one time Job Corpsmen in Menifee County searched (according to the *Menifee County Journal*) "an area from Sky Bridge and Rock Bridge westward along the Red River to Raven Rock, Court House Rock and Indian Creek where they have found several of the landmarks."[51] And a "mining and exploring" company searched in Wolfe County.

Years ago, the Swift mania cost one man his health, and after his death his widow returned to the search, squandering her fortune and her remaining years in futile pursuit of the treasure.[52] The legend of "John Swift" had struck again.

If, as the geological evidence indicates, Swift found no great veins of silver, it follows that the *Journal* is a fabrication. Putting aside the "cover-for-piracy" theory (which is a very leaky boat), we come to another. In *Silver Fleece*, Kidwell states, "thousands of transactions in real estate have hinged around the probability that it abounded with the abundant source of the Swift mines."[53] Isn't it conceivable the document was created for use in land schemes? It does appear it was later used for such a purpose. But, as I intend to demonstrate, there is a further possibility.

Swift says he marked a tree with "the symbols of a compass [some versions read "compasses"], trowel and square."[54] These *symbols* are meaningless in any but a single context: A combined *compass* (a drawing compass, or "pair of compasses") and *square* comprise the emblem of the "secret" society, Freemasonry. The *trowel* is the symbol of the Freemason's craft.

Freemasonry, or Masonry, is a benevolent society. It is not, Masons state, a "secret society" but a "society with secrets." First carried to America in the early eighteenth century, it has been defined as "a peculiar system of morality veiled in allegory and illustrated by symbols."[55]

Swift says he marked various trees and rocks with symbols which he referred to as "curious marks" and again as "peculiar marks." He identified one location of buried treasure with "a symbol of a triangle." Not *just* a triangle, but a *symbol*—one important in Masonry. Another Masonic symbol is the "Broad Arrow," also represented in the *Journal;* and there are many others.[56]

In the Masonic ritual of the Entered Apprentice, or First Degree, is the statement that there is "nothing more fervent than heated charcoal, it will melt the most obdurate metals."[57] Similarly, in the *Journal* Swift states, "We were able to make charcoal in large quantities, for our use in smelting the ore."[58]

The *Journal* continues in this vein (no pun intended): As part of the allegory, Swift claims that, when he left the "richest mine" for the last time, he "walled it up with masonry form."[59] Otherwise an unlikely expression, we need only capitalize "masonry" to see that this says, in effect, that the meaning has been concealed or "veiled" in Masonic fashion. It may be read with a knowing wink.

Now, among the essential elements of any true Masonic group are these: "a legend or allegory relating to the building of King Solomon's Temple" and "symbolism based on the stonemason's trade."[60] Masonry incorporates many legends of King Solomon, his masons, and the building of the temple. Indeed, the Masonic Lodge is held to represent some part of Solomon's Temple.[61] The lodge is oriented east and west, with east regarded as the most sacred of the cardinal points.[62]

Thus it is that our allegorist, "Swift," places his furnace in a "rockhouse that faces the east." From the rockhouse, he says, "facing the east you can see two monument rocks" (two tall rock pillars).[63] These are coincident with the Masonic/Solomonic "two great pillars" symbolizing Strength and Establishment.[64]

The remote and fabled mines, the fleet of ships (which supposedly bore Swift's silver to the "trade of the seas"), even the corral for horses, all tally with Solomon, his fabled mines (in "Ophir"), his great fleet, trade, and stables. Just as Swift refers to his "occupation as a silver-smith," Masons extol Solomon's Master Mason (whom they call Hiram Abif)—a smith, a craftsman in precious metals. And, like Swift, who supposedly found so much silver he could not transport all of it, Solomon "made silver to be in Jerusalem as stones."[65]

The Swift story admirably teaches its moral about the futility of "laying up treasures." It is not a true story but a parable in the form of a legend "veiled in allegory." In the *Journal*, Swift states the story's moral in a philosophical monologue: He says, in part, that "the works of man are always unfinished and unsatisfactory" and that "the life of man should be at some period turned about for reflection on God."[66]

Let us unveil a bit more. When Swift allegedly returned, years later, his blindness prevented him from relocating his treasure. This is the punchline of the allegory. In Masonry—which has been called the "Great Light"—light symbolizes enlightenment. (Swift says that from the "richest mine" you could "see a hole through the cliff and see the sky beyond." He called this formation "The Lighthouse."[67] In contrast, applicants for the Degrees of Masonry are first required to enter the lodge, like Swift, in *complete blindness*.[68] The "all-seeing eye" (depicted, for example, on the back of a dollar bill) is a prime Masonic symbol.[69]

Not only Swift's furnace but his "richest mine" was in a cave. He and his men camped in another. And he had rich stores of silver (walled up with "masonry form") "hidden in the great cavern . . . which fact was known to no living soul beyond our company."[70] (Like Masons, the members of Swift's "company" were "sworn to secrecy.") To this end, we should note that caves or "Clefts of the Rocks" figure prominently in Masonic symbolism. Too, there is the Masonic legend of the "Secret Vault," Solomon's subterranean depository of certain great secrets.[71]

The Masonic rites of the Third Degree feature a quest after such vague secrets (specifically "that which is lost") which, in the end, *remain lost.* [72] That, precisely, is the simple plot of the Swift legend. A "sea captain" figures in that Degree, and it will come as no surprise to learn that Swift states, "I became captain of a ship."

The parallels go on and on. Swift's landmarks include a "Lookout Rock," "Hanging Rock," and "Remarkable Rocks," including the two pillars or "Monument Rocks" previously noted. In Masonry, "Landmarks"—originally stone pillars for boundaries— are symbols distinguishing Masons from others. [73]

Various directions from the furnace are given in distances of "three miles." For example, "We carried the ore three miles to the furnace;" Furnace Creek forks "about three miles below the furnace;" again, "North of the furnace about three miles is a large hill." In Masonry, *three miles* represents a "Cable Tow's Length" which is "symbolic of the scope of a man's reasonable ability." [74]

The preceding only begins the possibilities. Such Masonic concepts as "The Conclusion of the Whole Matter," "The Camp," "The Contention among Brethren," "Treasure Room," "Cardinal Points" (of the Compass), "Circumnambulation," "Darkness to Light," "Weary Sojourners," and "Distressed Worthy Brother" all seem to have definite counterparts in the allegorical Swift "Journal." So do such symbols as the crescent moon, grapevine, laurel, crown, and others. [75]

There are historically dubious points in the *Journal* which are probably directly attributable to allegory. Arthur Edward Waite points out that "the significance is in the allegory and not in any point of history which may lie behind it." [76]

At least one dubious historical point is instructive. Swift refers to Indians "called Meccas." (Note the qualification that they were "called" that.) Although there was no such tribe, Henson guesses that "Meccas" or "Macces" may be a corruption of Mequechakes, a tribe of Shawnees. [77] On the other hand, in Masonic lore a copyist error appears with reference to "Maacha" (which is part of the Solomonic legend); Masons were referred to in the early charges and laws as "Maccones"; and the heroic Jewish family of Maccabees also figures in Masonry. [78]

I had a hunch that the allegorist might attempt to play games with numbers, especially since Masons make symbolic use of them. Swift's phrase, "reflection on God," suggested a look in the Bible. In four chapters of Isaiah—37, 56, 38, 2; indicated by the degrees and minutes of latitude—are to be found an amazing number of passages paralleling the Swift story. In Isaiah 2, for example, is this: "Their land also is full of silver and gold [Swift lists both silver and gold as part of his treasure], neither is there any end of their treasures" (Isa. 2:7). In this one chapter alone are allusions to Solomon, ships, idols cast of silver (Swift cast coins and silver bars), plus a phrase (adopted by Masons!): "Clefts of the Rocks" (Isa. 2:13, 16, 20-21).[79]

So many parallels with the Swift allegory! Reading and understanding these passages from Isaiah (containing symbolism adopted by Freemasonry) help us to understand the moral of the Swift allegory. After almost two hundred years, the key to the "cipher" has been broken.

One of the problems allegories present is that of interpretation. It has not been my intent to twist facts to fit a theory. I can only repeat that the *Journal* itself *demands* comparison with Freemasonry since so many Masonic symbols are expressly given therein. Clearly these elements—compasses, square and trowel—refer to Masonry *to the exclusion of any other meaning.*

This does not mean "Swift" was a Mason, of course, since his very existence is doubtful. Nor does it *necessarily* mean that the original version of the *Journal* (long lost!) contained such symbolism—although every indication is that it did. In the following section I will detail evidence which strongly suggests the author's intent, as well as indications of who he was and when the allegory was drafted. As we shall see, John Filson is conspicuously present in the Swift affair.

The earliest documented reference to Swift's silver mines is this land record of May 17, 1788:

Robert Breckenridge and John Filson as Tenants in Common Enters 1000 acres of land upon the balance of a Treasury Warrant No. 10,117 about sixty or seventy miles North Eastwardly from Martins Cabbins in Powells Valley to Include a silver mine which was Improved about 17 years ago by a Certain man named Swift at said mine, wherein the said Swift Reports he has extracted from the oar a Considerable quantity of Silver some of which he made into Dollars and left at or near the mine, together with the apparatus for making the same, the Land to be in a Square and the lines to run at the Cardinal Points of the Compass including the mine in the Centre as near as may be.[80]

Filson is of course the famous Kentuckian who produced the first map of the state together with the first history, *The Discovery, Settlement and Present State of Kentucke,* 1784, in which he wrote, "Iron ore and lead are found in abundance, but we do not hear of any silver or gold mines as yet discovered."[81]

Now Filson's book, and the statements in it, contained endorsement by "Daniel Boon, Levi Todd, James Harrod." The opinions of these exceedingly knowledgeable men should have been the best obtainable, and they hadn't even *heard,* in all their travels, an allegation of silver mines. Yet in four years the name "Swift" had come to light, his mine had been located, and it was Filson who had gotten lucky. Weigh the odds.

There is, in fact, *absolutely no evidence of the "Swift Mines" legend prior to the 1788 Filson document.* It would be interesting if we could ask John Filson how he had located the mine. But since we cannot, we *can* look at the man and his activities in hope of clues. They are forthcoming.

Consider this portrait of Filson by William Masterson of Rice University:

His was a strange personality. Fiercely acquisitive, he secured, on paper at least, over 12,000 acres of land. For gain he plunged into arduous schemes, sued and was sued, and endured all the hardships of an incredibly savage frontier. For gain, despite pious explanations to the contrary, he wrote his book and drew his map, the products of hours and days of interviews, travel, and technical skill. He was not friendly and was possessed of a deadly duality of impatience and pompousness. Like his map he lacked perspective—the map at the eastern and western ends, the man in any direction that touched upon personal standing and relationships. Except for the map and book he was in all his endeavors, including his one known courtship, almost ludicrously unsuccessful.

He died penniless.[82]

Masterson added, "Yet Filson's very energy attracts." His frontier travels were extensive. He taught at Transylvania, studied medicine and untold other subjects, conducted countless interviews, surveyed roads, wrote poetry and created sundry documents at the request of others, helped to found a city and attempted to found a seminary (tuition: "one half cash the other property").[83]

If the reader suspects I am about to "accuse" Filson of perpetrating the Swift hoax, he is partly right: I wish to suggest that there are numerous *indications*—if not conclusive evidence—that he did so. Let us examine the indications.

First, there are Masonic symbols and allusions in the text of Filson's land record, but we cannot be certain they are not purely coincidental. For example, "Cardinal Points of the Compass" is a definite Masonic term, while on the other hand nothing precludes a non-Mason's innocent use of the expression in a deed. Presently we shall look at Filson's Masonic ties; first, let's consider other evidence.

In that pioneer era of Kentucky, Filson was one of the very, very few who could have met *all* the necessary requirements for drafting the *Journal*. His scholarship, and his ability to write and to create maps would obviously have been necessary talents together with his excellent knowledge of Kentucky. There was nothing in his mixed character to preclude a motive—and several motives present themselves.

Putting words into "Swift's" mouth would have been child's play for Filson, for after all, he had given these words to Daniel Boone in a ghostwritten account of the hero's exploits: "The aspect of these cliffs is so wild and horrid, that it it impossible to behold them without terror. The spectator is apt to imagine that nature had formerly suffered some violent convulsion; and that these are the dismembered remains of the dreadful shock; the ruins, not of Persepolis or Palmyra, but of the world!"[84] Exclamation mark indeed! Anyone who could bestow upon a backwoodsman such an instant education would have no trouble saddling an untutored "sea captain" with a phrase like "deeming it imprudent."

Filson occasionally sounds like the surveyor he was, with a string of "thences": "thence down the same to the mouth; thence up the Ohio,"[85] as if he were drafting a deed of land. Swift writes: "We . . . came to Leesburg, thence to Winchester, thence to Littles, thence to Fort Pitt."[86]

"Swift's" division of his manuscript into sections—"Description of the Mines and County," "Ore South of the Furnace," etc.— parallels Filson's treatment of his book: "Situation and Boundaries," "Soil and Produce," etc. Filson evidently patterned his miscellany after Jefferson's *Notes on the State of Virginia*, manuscript copies of which were in circulation *after 1781*.[87] Let us hope no one suggests Jefferson copied "Swift!"

After relating some of the early history of exploration, Filson (following Jefferson's approach) described the boundaries. He began, "Kentucke is situated, in its central part, near the latitude of 38° north, and 85° west longitude, and lying within the fifth climate. . . . It is bounded on the north by great Sandy-creek. . . ."[88] And "Swift," after recounting his comings and goings, gives his "Description of the Mines and Country," including, as previously noted, the latitude and longitude. He says the furnace is on "a long rocky branch."[89] Also throughout, there is a similarity of both style and outlook.

But did Filson have the particularly literary (and not just journalistic) turn of mind necessary to contrive a complex allegory replete with clever symbolism? The answer is emphatically yes. He was, for one thing, a poet. But an example of his genius for cleverness is found in the name he proposed for the city he helped to found. He called it "Losantiville." As he explained, "L for Licking River; os, Latin for mouth; anti, Greek for opposite; and ville, French for city." Read *backward*, it translates as "city opposite the mouth of the Licking"! Although later the name was changed to Cincinnati, some Filson notes have survived to reveal his pedantic virtuosity.[90]

Filson may well have been a Freemason. Certainly some of his closest associates and contemporaries were. Significantly, in 1788 (the year in which the *Journal* was probably created, or at least finished), *Filson was actually living in the home of a prominent Mason,* Col. Robert Patterson[91]—soon to be a Filson partner in founding "Losantiville." It was in this significant year of 1788, on November 17, that the "first lodge west of the Alleghanies," Masonic Lodge No. 25 at Lexington, was issued a charter.[92] The date of the application for the charter is unknown, but surely it was some time (weeks or even months) before. Unfortunately, the names of the charter members of Lodge No. 25 are irretrievably lost,[93] but it does seem that while plans were being made to establish the lodge, Filson—living in Patterson's home—was close at hand. And it is very likely that, with his extraordinary curiosity and his admiration for Masons, he sought membership in the society.

While there is no direct proof the "Swift Silver Mines" allegory was adopted for actual use by Masons, Freemasonry is, after all, a "society with secrets." Further, many appendant orders of the brotherhood have flourished briefly before passing into obscurity. If Filson had written the allegory (say at the request of Patterson), it might simply have suffered the same fate as "Losantiville." Or possibly another fate, which I will touch on presently.

Filson's talents frequently earned him requests to write documents for others. For example, it was he who drafted the petition to Congress on behalf of the families at Post St. Vincent pleading for military protection (and for the establishment of a "permanent land office here, for the purpose of obtaining valid rights to lands."[94] Land was a Filson obsession and he dwells on explaining how to acquire it in his book). He also wrote the announcement for a proposed Lexington seminary (a "bizarre" document, as his biographer admits)[95] as well as the prospectus for the proposed settlement of "Losantiville." It was *at the request of Colonel Patterson* that Filson set to the task of conjuring up that "veiled" name.[96]

In mid-1788 Filson wrote to his brother, who was being harassed by Filson's creditors, a letter most revealing of his character. He said, in part, "I have supported a good credit here [Lexington], and have enough to support me. I resumed my studies last winter . . . and this spring have begun to study Physic with Doctr Slater. . . . Two years I study, as soon as my study is finished I am to be married, which will be greatly to our advantage. Stand it out 2 years my dear brother, you shall have negroes to wait of you."[97] The letter was written only ten days after Filson recorded his supposed discovery of the silver mine, yet he makes no reference to it! Did he *know* the mine was only legendary?

He did not travel to the mine. Instead he headed in the opposite direction. A month later, at Beargrass (near Louisville), he composed a poem, indicating he had been spurned in love, and threatening suicide.[98]

By September 23, Filson had arrived at "Losantiville" with his two partners: Colonel Patterson and Matthias Denman of New Jersey, who had obtained the land. After the preliminary survey, Filson disappeared. He was rumored killed by Indians, although his body was never found, and another surveyor, Israel Ludlow, took his place in the partnership. John Walton, Filson's biographer, states, "Years later, sworn testimony was given that these men ransacked Filson's trunk and destroyed his papers in order to defraud his heirs."[99] Could the Swift allegory have been among the papers in the ransacked trunk?

A great deal of circumstantial evidence connects Filson with the "Swift" manuscript. *Someone* certainly contrived it, and at every turn, Filson is suspiciously present, with Col. Robert Patterson not far behind.

After Filson's death, the records are silent as to "Swift's Mine" for more than two years. Then there is this entry: "April 1791. Eli Cleveland withdraws his entry of 200 acres made January 5, 1791 on Warrant No. 15132. Eli Cleveland and John Morton enters 1483 acres of land on two Treasury Warrants No. 15132 and 12128 on a branch of Red River to Include an Old Camp in the Center where there is some old troughs at said Camp by the branch side. The said Camp is a place difficult of access Supposed to be Swift's Old Camp and others including a mine said to be occupied formerly by said Swift and others."[100] John Morton (who later became a banker) was a Mason,[101] and his partner, Eli Cleveland, may have been. Cleveland was closely linked with Colonel Patterson since they were (at roughly this time) fellow magistrates of Fayette County.[102]

In two more years these county lawmen were to learn of a bizarre and tragic episode in the "Swift" saga. Col. James Harrod, prominent as the founder of Harrodsburg, was reported murdered after being lured on a search for the mines[103] by a man named Bridges—a man with whom Harrod "had a lawsuit about property."[104] In his little book, Filson had called Col. Harrod "a gentleman of veracity."[105]

Several years later, in 1815, Col. Wm. McMillan of Clark County, with eleven other men, formed a "company"[106] to search for the Swift mines. McMillan possessed, at least according to later legend, the "original" *Journal* and map. As to the latter: "From notes relating to it, it must have been in cipher, for finding the place appeared to depend upon the phases of the moon or signs of the zodiac or some mysterious combination of circumstances, perhaps never revealed."[107] Had the map survived, only then might we do more than guess that the "cipher" was composed of Masonic symbols.

I did succeed in establishing that "William McMillin" was active in Clark County,[108] and that a "Wm. McMillan" was at "Losantiville" in 1788. He arrived with a party brought by Colonel Patterson shortly after Filson's reported death.[109] This much is clear: Any further clues concerning "Swift's Mines" will be unearthed—not in the soil of Kentucky—but in the neglected dust of archives.

Recommended Works

Brunvand, Jan Harold. *The Study of American Folklore: An Introduction*. 2d ed. New York: Norton, 1978. Scholarly treatment of the subject with important discussion of the qualities of "true folklore," including variant texts, oral transmission, and traditional form.

Cavendish, Richard, ed. *Legends of the World: A Cyclopedia of the Enduring Myths, Legends, and Sagas of Mankind*. New York: Schocken Books, 1982. Compendium (arranged geographically) of the dominant legends of the world's major cultures.

Cohen, Daniel. "El Dorado: Home of the Gilded Phantom," chap. 10 of *Mysterious Places*. New York: Dodd, Mead, 1969. Story of Spanish conquistadors' search for the South American "city of the gilded man."

Dorson, Richard M. *American Folklore*. Chicago: Univ. of Chicago Press, 1959. Highly readable survey of American folklore, tracing its forms and content against the background of United States history.

―――. *Folklore and Folklife: An Introduction*. Chicago: Univ. of Chicago Press, 1972. Broad treatise on various aspects of folklore, the oral traditions as well as folk customs.

Fletcher, William. *Talking Your Roots: A Family Guide to Tape Recording and Videotaping Oral History*. Washington, D.C.: Privately printed, 1983. Thorough how-to book on conducting a "Life History Interview" with an elderly person; includes sections on family history and historical events.

Grissim, John. *The Lost Treasure of the Concepcion*. New York: William Morrow, 1980. Story of failed and successful searches for shipwrecked Spanish galleon's treasure, including too-brief description of quest for logbook that pinpointed site. Provides interesting comparisons and contrasts with "Swift" treasure searches.

Ketchum, Alton. *Uncle Sam: The Man and the Legend*. New York: Hill and Wang, 1959. Story of how Samuel "Uncle Sam" Wilson, meat packer for Government during War of 1812, became original for American symbol.

Morrison, Joan, and Charlotte Fox Zabusky. *American Mosaic: The Immigrant Experience in the Words of Those Who Lived It*. New York: E.P. Dutton, 1980. Collection of oral histories of American immigrants, both famous and otherwise.

D. Boone Riddles

Investigated with John F. Fischer

Artifacts (products of human workmanship) are tangible survivals of the past. Both prehistoric artifacts (such as Stone Age tools) and historic ones (like spinning wheels or millstones) can help fill gaps in man's knowledge. States one writer:

History, the total story of mankind, comes to life for us when we can see and study the treasures man has left behind in his journey through time. The word "treasure" usually evokes images of jewels and gold and silver plate set with precious stones, or ancient chests bursting with coins, pearls, or uncut diamonds. Yet the smallest finds uncovered on an archaeological dig—a single stone weapon, some shreds of food left in a tomb a thousand years ago, or the hub and broken spokes of an ancient wheel—all of little intrinsic value—may be treasures, too. Treasures of the mind, that is, for each could be a link to man's past, leading to the discovery of new and unexpected wealth of understanding of human history.[1]

Conversely, spurious artifacts are antitreasures, capable of distorting the historical picture (and are thus analogous to a sociopath's act of vandalism). At least, they may divert scholars from more profitable study. Consider, for example, the case of the infamous Kensington Stone.

In 1898, on his farm near Kensington, Minnesota, Olof Ohman claimed to have unearthed a curious stone that was entwined in the roots of an aged tree. Bearing what proved to be a runic inscription (runes are medieval Scandinavian letters), the 200-pound slab of greywacke became the subject of protracted controversy. If genuine, the inscription—telling of a fourteenth-century Viking penetration of the North American interior—would require the rewriting of American prehistory, specifically that of pre-

Columbian exploration. Translated, the inscription reads: "Eight Goths and twenty-two Norwegians upon an exploring journey from Vinland to the west. We had camped by two skerries [i.e., rocky islets] one day's journey north from this stone. We were fishing one day; when we returned home [we] found ten men red with blood and dead. A.V.M.[Ave Virgo Maria (Hail, Virgin Mary)] save [us] from evil. [We] have ten men by the sea to look after our vessel fourteen [or forty-one] days' travel from this island. Year 1362."[2]

Although Norwegian-American writer Hjalmar Holand spent much of his life attempting to authenticate the Kensington Stone, scholars demonstrated that the alleged fourteenth-century Scandinavian dialect contained countless anachronisms. Indeed, the writing was a thousand years out of style.

Finally in 1976 Walter and Anna Josephine Gran reported that their father, John, had confessed to them his involvement in the hoax. He, together with Ohman and schoolteacher Sven Fogelblad (who was knowledgeable about runes), had carved the bogus inscription as a prank to show up some of the more learned members of their community.[3]

Supposedly even earlier than the purportedly fourteenth-century inscription on the Kensington Stone are Peruvian carvings depicting complex scientific activities of many centuries ago. The stones, which are in the collection of Dr. Janvier Cabrera Darquea of Ica, Peru, portray ancient Peruvian Indians performing complex medical operations such as brain surgery and heart transplants, gazing through telescopes, and the like. Erich von Däniken (discussed in chapter 2 regarding his postulated extraterrestrial link to the Nazca drawings) sees the Ica carvings as further proof of his ancient astronaut "theory."

Alas for fantasy mongers, the stone carvings are spurious, the creation—according to a BBC television team—of a local Ican artisan named Basilio. To "age" the stones artificially, Basilio applies a coating of black boot polish before firing them (appropriately enough) in donkey dung.[4]

Fake artifacts in the form of religious relics proliferated in the middle ages. Associated with the ancient prophets, the relics represented attempts to establish their lives historically[5] and enhance the church's influence. Created, sold, and enshrined were such items as Moses' rod, Enoch's slippers, and Joseph's "coat of many colors."

Relics of Jesus' parents were more common. Items from Joseph's carpentry shop—his hammer as well as objects worked on by the young Jesus—were "discovered." Pilgrims visited the Holy House in which Mary had lived at the time of the Annunciation; it was located at Loretto, Italy, where it had been miraculously transported.[6]

Alleged relics of the Crucifixion were especially plentiful. It was said that there were enough fragments of the True Cross to build a ship. Three European churches had the single lance which had pierced Jesus' side. And there were some forty "genuine" shrouds, including the notorious Holy Shroud of Turin (discussed in a later chapter) bearing the portrait-like "imprint" of Jesus' body. (As well, there were such nonartifact relics as vials of Jesus' blood and Mary's breast milk, skulls of the three Wise Men, and so on; three churches had the very corpse of Mary Magdalen.)[7]

With the Renaissance, the revival of learning following the medieval period, there awakened an interest in the acquisition of artifacts: old coins, ancient statuary and other objets d'art, arms and armor, manuscript books, and similar rarities. Public and private collections grew, and from the latter fine arts museums developed.[8] Forgers followed close behind, and their nefarious activities have continued unabated. For example, in 1931, a British authority stated that "one does not require an expert, but an actuary, to tell the collector of English furniture that, in one year, more is shipped to America than could have been made in the whole of the eighteenth century."[9] More recently it was pointed out that

most of the "antiquities" which eager Italian policemen confiscate today are fakes. In February 1968, Rome police broke up what they said was an international ring that had dealt in clandestine antiquities for more than ten years. In an abandoned lime kiln just a few miles outside of Rome they found a cache of the ring's goods: more than two hundred pieces of Etruscan and Greek pottery, Roman carved heads, jewelry, vases, bronze statues, ancient coins. Some of the treasure was already boxed for shipment abroad. Officials studied it all carefully and pronounced some ten to thirty percent of it genuine and valuable; the rest of the hundreds of pieces were fakes. Police estimated that gullible buyers in Belgium, Switzerland, Germany and the United States had been deceived through the years by this one ring of dealers and shippers.[10]

Some appreciation for what is required of a good forger can be seen from the modus operandi of Italian forger Alfredo Fioravanti and his friends, three members of the Riccardi family. They produced terra-cotta statues of Etruscan warriors that—for forty years—fooled experts at the New York City's Metropolitan Museum of Art.

To make the Etruscan figures they worked slowly from catalogue illustrations of Etruscan ware in Italian and foreign museums. They were careful never to excite suspicion by copying a known statue exactly. They always adapted slightly or changed size and proportions. They used the same native clay that the ancient Etruscans had used, and they modeled their figures from the feet up, as the Etruscans had done. When they began making really big pieces, however, they had a problem. Their ovens, designed for firing pottery only, were small, only about four feet high. The Etruscans had had gigantic ovens which could take life-size figures. There was only one solution for Fioravanti and the Riccardis: they would have to break their big statues before firing them, and then fire them in pieces.[11]

The range of specializations applied to artifact fakery is impressive. There are prehistoric stone implements (Lewis Erickson's flint fakes adorned the collections of experienced archaeologists prior to a professor's exposé of 1900);[12] Old Masters' paintings (Han van Meegeren's "Vermeers" seemed too good to be fakes, until he painted another before witnesses);[13] antique sculptures (Alceo Dossena, an Italian stonemason, manufactured remarkable Greek-, Roman-, Gothic-, and Renaissance-style fakes for dealers who passed them off as authentic);[14] Etruscan pottery (enterprising forgers sometimes planted their new pots in Etruscan tombs to "age" then "sold" the "unopened" tombs to gullible foreign dealers);[15] "ancient" coins (they fill cardboard boxes in Rome's *belli arti* section flea market);[16] bronze tablets,[17] and so on: "old" Spanish armor[18] "stradivarius" violins,[19] "antique" furniture,"[20] "Tiffany glass,[21] "folk" art (such as early copper weather vanes[22] and scrimshaw whaling relics);[23] "early" samplers,[24] "pre-Columbian" figures.[25] In many cases, honest reproductions are simply being converted to forgeries by amateurs who remove telltale imprints and artificially age the pieces.

Just as the production of forged artifacts can require specialized knowledge, so can their detection. For example, according to a British expert in antique furniture:

To explain the tools of the various periods and the evidence of their use is impossible in a book. Such knowledge can only be acquired in the workshop. Yet it must be obvious that tools, which were utterly unknown in the eighteenth century or earlier, cannot have been used on the furniture of that period, and if one finds indications of the circular saw, for instance, it must be evidence of modern origin. Conversely, one would hardly look for signs of the adze—the tool of the primitive carpenter—in the furniture of Georgian days. Side by side with this acquaintance of tools goes the knowledge of woods. There are nearly thirty different kinds of mahogany at the present day, and more than half that number of walnut. There is English oak of at least two kinds, oak from Riga, Holland, France, Germany, Italy, Austria, America and even Japan. Even with English oak, at the present day, the timber is not that from the age-old trees such as was used in the sixteenth and seventeenth centuries; these have been cut down long ago.[26]

Yet the need for detailed knowledge does not mean that only specialists can function as historical investigators. It merely means that—at an appropriate stage in the investigation of a questioned artifact—a specialist *may* need to be consulted.

The antique detective's first step is simply to recognize when an artifact may be questionable. For example in a piece of antique furniture, the presence, on the surface, of worm *channels*—rather than mere bored *holes*—is prima-facie evidence of spuriousness: that the piece was made from worm-eaten wood, with the furrows having been exposed by subsequent workmanship (e.g., by planing).[27] But in an important case the matter should be passed on to an expert.

Sometimes the investigator's preliminary inspection can uncover evidence that can resolve a question of authenticity. For instance, the author was asked to examine two large photographs of Abraham Lincoln. One showed a crease mark and the dark margins of a water stain, yet upon its removal from its frame it was seen that the paper was not itself creased or stained; therefore the print was a *reproduction* of a photo which had such damage. The other photograph bore the embossment (eventually deciphered by using oblique light) of a New York studio, whereas research showed that that particular image was made by Mathew Brady; again a reproduction was indicated.

Another case, however, did require calling in an expert. A schoolteacher had brought me a large bullet-shaped object found in a Kentucky creek. He wanted to know: Was it a Civil War artillery projectile? Its covering of heavy brass foil seemed to render that possibility unlikely, but I was eventually able to locate an expert on Civil War munitions and to send him detailed measurements and close-up photographs. He concluded that the unidentified object not only failed to match any known Civil War projectile but that its proportions would have rendered it ballistically unstable (i.e., it could not have flown straight).[28]

Whenever a significant artifact is questioned, the historical detective must attempt to devise an investigative strategy capable of resolving the issue. He may make (or commission to be made) a stylistic study, a detailed examination of workmanship, scientific tests of materials, or other appropriate analyses, including an investigation of provenance (the history or chain of ownership of an item). Sometimes a single, incontrovertible fact is fatal to authenticity, as when x-rays revealed that a triptych—painted and gilded in fifteenth-century Sienese style—had modern hinges and machine-made nails.[29]

But more often it is an array of factors that is offered in evidence. That was the approach John Fischer and I used in investigating some artifacts supposedly inscribed by the knife of Kentucky's famed frontiersman, Daniel Boone.

More than two decades ago, men searching for eastern Kentucky's legendary "lost silver mines" came upon a huge rock shelter (or cliff overhang) in the Daniel Boone National Forest, roughly three miles northeast of Natural Bridge State Resort Park. Within the shelter were wooden troughs and other relics of human habitation, including a crude "hut." (Figure 11). This has been assembled from poles suspended across large rocks, and upon these makeshift rafters had been laid rows of old-fashioned shakes (split shingles like those used for the roofs of log cabins). Inside the hut the men discovered a board (another shake) with the carved inscription, "D. BooN" (see Figure 12).

Although the treasure hunters kept their discovery secret for some four years, they finally made it public. But then few took the matter seriously until an elderly professor from Eastern Kentucky University arrived on the scene, asserted the "camp" was surely associated with Boone's explorations, and removed the inscribed plank for safekeeping. Subsequently, forest officials obtained the board, enclosed the rock shelter with a fence, and attempted to authenticate the site.[30]

Figure 11. Ranger Don Fig at the Boone "Hut" in 1967. (Photo courtesy U.S. Forest Service.)

Media coverage in the late sixties reported on the "cabin," as it was sometimes called, with astonishing inaccuracy. For example, the rock shelter was described as a "cave,"[31] and the board's inscription was given variously as "D. BooN," "D. boon," or "D. Boone."[32] Unidentified "scholars" reportedly "examined the lettering and declared it had been made by Boone."[33]

Of various notions about the hut's construction, one was that it had been fashioned by "John Swift" who had supposedly mined silver in the region in the 1760s. Other suggestions were that Boone

Figure 12. Board from "Hut" inscribed "D. BooN" displayed at Forest Service Office in Winchester, Kentucky. (Photo by John F. Fischer.)

had shared the camp with "Swift," or had later discovered "Swift's" site and adopted it for his base camp. Some took the carved board at face value and assumed Boone was alone responsible. Still other theories held that the hut was constructed by miners producing niter for gunpowder during the War of 1812, or that it was built even later by moonshiners.[34]

Obviously much depended on the "D. BooN" inscription. Whether or not it was authentic was a question John Fischer and I addressed in a two-year investigation that grew to include a number of questionable Boone artifacts—not only the "hut" but various tree and rock inscriptions, as well as carvings on rifles and other supposed possessions of the famous Kentuckian.

As we learned from studying many authentic Boone letters and documents, the evidence is that Boone always rendered the family name with a uniform spelling. Our conclusion supports that of Kentucky historian George W. Ranck, who observed in 1901," all the original autographs of the famous woodsman or *fac-similes* of them that the writer has even seen show the name with the final 'e.' "[35] In its issue of December 23, 1934, the *Louisville Courier-Journal* sagely advised that Boone's lack of education had been exaggerated and that, apparently, "he knew how to spell his own name." The distinguished New York autograph expert, Charles Hamilton, author of *Great Forgers and Famous Fakes*, agrees. As he pointed out to us, Boone's "handwriting and spelling were remarkably consistent."[36]

As a result, proliferating inscriptions bearing the explorer's name can often be dismissed on purely orthographic grounds. According to Boone biographer Lawrence Elliott, "unhappily for a number of historical societies still cherishing segments of ancient tree bark with what is said to be Boone's carved inscriptions— 'D. Boon killa bar on this tree 1773,' or, 'D. Boon cilled a bar on tree in the year 1760'—he did know how to spell his name properly."[37]

The first of the examples Elliott cites—found near Long Island, Tennessee—is additionally discredited by its use of the present-tense form "kill" for the past tense *killed*.[38] Boone generally used tense forms correctly. In fact, in a letter dated May 7, 1789, Boone wrote of hearing that Indians "have kiled" some people, and again that "5 pursons Were Certinly kiled" a few days earlier.[39]

The use of "cilled" in the second example, found on a large tree at Fancy Gap, Virginia, is not only a non-Boone spelling but is not a very credible rendering in any case. And as to the spelling "bar," we found entries in Boone's account books—authentic entries in the frontiersman's own handwriting—for "Bear Skines."[40]

Again, a misspelling of the frontiersman's name betrays the spuriousness of an inscription on a slab of beech tree in the warehouse of the Kentucky Historical Society. Reportedly from Clay County, Kentucky, it reads, "D. Boon" and bears the date "1775."[41] Another obviously fake inscription—"D. Boon campt here"—supposedly came from a tree "near the mouth of one of the caves that he explored."[42] Yet another, "D. Boon," scribed in the chinking of a log house in Harrison County, Kentucky, was discovered when it was being renovated by its owner, Ernie Covington.[43]

The inscription "D. BOON 1776" has turned up on beech trees in Tennessee[44] and Kentucky[45] as well as on an aspen in Idaho![46] A small book was written on the latter. Amusingly, its author once thought the carving a fake because she had been misinformed that the spelling was "BOONE"; when she saw it was actually "BOON," she decided it might be genuine after all! And when tree experts determined the carving was made about 1895, and was therefore a fake, she came up with an incredible hypothesis: She decided some trapper or prospector had likely seen "the old Boone inscription after the original tree had died, and decided to carve the exact name and date on a similar tree in order to pass on a message for another century."[47]

We see then, that authentic specimens of Boone's writing—as Elliott says, "his undisputed signatures on letters, deeds and claims"—always have the final "e."[48] It is only with the highly questionable artifacts, which often bear additional signs of faking, that one finds the other spelling. At least one source for that persistent error is Boone's so-called autobiography, actually written by John Filson, which was popular in the last century and which gave the backwoodsman's name as "Col. Daniel Boon."[49] In turn, repeated publicizing of the fake inscriptions no doubt caused the misconception to become even more widespread.

Nevertheless, in an attempt to justify particular instances of the misspelling, some writers have offered an ingenious explanation. According to one such writer, "Boone did not begin spelling his name with the 'e' until after he moved to Boonesborough in 1775."[50] Unfortunately, since there is no documentary evidence for that assertion, the argument is necessarily circular, running something like this: "Tree carvings prove the explorer formerly spelled his name as 'Boon'; therefore, that spelling adds credibility to the tree carvings." Actually, entries in Boone's own family bible refute the assertion of an early "Boon" spelling.[51]

As might be expected, however, not all hoaxers have omitted the final "e." In 1983, I was able to inspect a sandstone rock that was reportedly found on a Madison County, Kentucky, farm in 1900.[52] Above the "D. BOONE" name was carved the year, "1765." That date brands the inscription a fake because, historians agree, Boone never entered Kentucky until 1767, as he himself told Filson for the "autobiography."[53]

Another example of the correct spelling but the wrong date is the carving on a section of an old tree that was cut down in 1932 in Iroquois Park in Louisville. Now in possesion of the Filson Club, it reads, "D. BOONE. KILL A BAR. 1803." Appended is a word that appears to read "ZOIS" but which has not been satisfactorily explained.[54] (See Figure 13.) But if the final word is puzzling, the matter of the carving's legitimacy is not: In addition to the non-Boone forms such as we have already discussed, the date brands the

Figure 13. The Boone tree in Louisville's Iroquois Park. (Photo courtesy The Filson Club.)

inscription a fake. In 1803, Daniel Boone was serving as a magistrate in Missouri where he had resided for a few years, and he would not return to Kentucky until about 1810.[55]

Then there are the "D.B." inscriptions presumed to have been made by Boone. Two so attributed once stood on opposite sides of Morgan County, Kentucky.[56] However, our research shows the possibility of mistaken identity: Some Blairs, including a David, had been early settlers of one of the locales,[57] and the family of Richard "Dickie" Burks —including a grandson, David Burkes— had lived in the other.[58] There is no independent proof that Boone ever visited either immediate area. It is, in fact, unlikely that he actually did.

Among many other "D.B." inscriptions was one found on a large tree above a "cave" (actually a rock shelter) where Boone supposedly wintered in 1769.[59] (This may be the same "D.B." carving preserved on a segment of bark in the Mansion Museum at Old Fort Harrod, Harrodsburg, Kentucky. It is captioned: "The initials D.B. cut by Daniel Boone on an oak tree above the cave where he spent the winter of 1769-70 in Kentucky.") However, author/historian Maria Thompson Daviess, on whose father's property the "cave" had been located, wrote that she "always had too much respect for D.B.'s good judgment to believe for an hour that he wintered in that one when so many more commodious caves and even hollow trees offered their hospitable shelter all around." She added, "As to the letters, the average boy is fond enough of climbing and cutting to make that much history." [60]

Among the best known of the "D.B." carvings is that on the stock of a rifle in the museum of the Kentucky Historical Society. That the initials are supposed to refer to the famous Kentuckian is clear from the inscription carved on the other side: "BOoNs bESt FREN." (See Figure 14.)

The inscription implies this was Boone's favorite rifle, whereas Boone reportedly referred to his trusty firearm as "old Tick-Licker." [61] He would not have carved "FREN" in any case: Rather, he spelled the word with the final "d," as in a letter to his sister-in-law in which he sent his affection to "all my frends." [62] The possessive form of his name is also wrong since he retained the final "e" there as well. For example, in a survey document in his handwriting he referred to "said Boones SW corner." [63]

Cut into the gunstock are also 15 notches—"for Indians shot," according to the man who sold the rifle to the historical society at the turn of the century. But Kentucky historian Winston Coleman stated, "I seriously doubt that Boone put the notches there. In the first place, those people thought too much of their guns to mutilate them." [64] Another historian, Bayless Hardin, agreed: It seems the custom of notching a pistol or rifle originated out West during "the Buffalo Bill era." [65]

Museum records inform that the rifle was acquired by the Commonwealth of Kentucky in 1900 from "Prof. Gilbert Walden" (Figure 15). No doubt that title "Professor" conjures up visions of a venerable historian, possibly even a Boone expert. Actually, a somewhat different impression comes from Walden's letter to the Governor of Kentucky in 1900. The bold letterhead reads: "CULTURE. ORATORY. PATRIOTISM. STORY. AND. SONG. AMERICA'S FAMOUS ELOCUTIONIST." Below, in large ornate letters is: "Gilbert Walden, Washington, D.C., Virginia, Texas, and Oklahoma." "Professor" Walden's photo dominates the letterhead. It shows him seated, dressed in western attire, with a rifle balanced on his knee and a pistol stuck in his belt. In bold letters is this additional list of his

Figure 14. Spelling of inscription on rifle stock is evidence of fakery. (Photo courtesy Kentucky Military History Museum.)

talents: "Noted Cow-boy Orator, Rough Rider, Scholar and Rifle Shot."

In a sprawling hand, the self-described "Scholar and Rifle Shot" wrote of the rifle:

It is about 140 years old, and was made for Boone by a famous gunsmith from N.C., named Graham, who lived on the Elkhorn in Ky., and made guns for many years after the Pioneers had moved away or died. I got it through the kindness of Dr. Percy de Bonay, of Tallulah Falls, Ga., who had gotten it from a gentleman in Louisville and who had found it through a newspaper article in a country paper in N.E. Kentucky.

It was given to an old trapper and friend of Boone named Dedman and kept in a mountaineer family for years. For a long time it was hidden away in an old closet until found. The people were nice and intelligent who had it, but poor, and they sold it to a Col. Ellis (I think) of Louisville and a friend of Dr. de Bonay's.[66]

If the rifle was indeed made when Walden claimed—circa 1760—it would be most unlikely to have actually belonged to Daniel Boone. That is because Boone's rifles, as well as his other possessions and those of his companions, were confiscated by the men's Indian captors in late 1769. The only weapon the men were allowed to take with them on their release was a small "trading gun."[67]

Another problem with Walden's story concerns his mention of the "newspaper article in a country paper in N.E. Kentucky." We found a photocopy of what must surely be the same old clipping in the files of the Kentucky Military History Museum. It is unidentified and undated and quotes an anonymous "gentleman from Eastern Kentucky." The man (who refers to himself with the royal "we") stated that he had an old rifle which was "said to have been" owned by Daniel Boone. He mentioned the fifteen notches and the "rude letters: BoONEs bEst FRIN." But the anonymous gentlemen gave a notably different record of the rifle's prior ownership.

The point here is not that "Professor" Walden intended to be deceptive in this regard. (After all, it was probably he who supplied the old clipping.) Rather, it is merely to show that the alleged provenance is even more tortuous and uncertain and unverifiable than has heretofore been reported.[68]

In short, the gun's provenance is confused and suspect, and the inscription is fraudulent. As forgery expert Charles Hamilton told us, shortly after he had exposed the "Hitler Diaries" as spurious on the basis of the handwriting, "I think the Kentucky Historical Society has a lot of nerve to display a remark [i.e., "BOoNs bESt FREN"] that even from this distance I can spy as a fake."[69]

In addition to this damning evidence, during our investigation we repeatedly heard doubts expressed about the rifle's antiquity. These came from a number of knowledgeable persons. A long-rifle expert who had once thoroughly examined the rifle branded it an obvious fake, and a collector of antique firearms agreed the rifle is of doubtful authenticity on stylistic grounds.[70]

Such expressions persuaded us to contact an independent expert, and we asked for a recommendation from Henry J. Kauffman of Lancaster, Pennsylvania, author of the important text, *The Pennsylvania-Kentucky Rifle* (1960). Since the rifle in question was alleged to have come from North Carolina, Mr. Kauffman suggested we contact John Bivins of the Museum of Early Southern Decorative Arts, in Winston-Salem, North Carolina, who readily agreed to assist us in our investigation.

In a subsequent letter, Mr. Bivins wrote:

Figure 15. "Professor" Gilbert Walden with his "Boon" rifle. (Photo courtesy Kentucky Military History Museum.)

Matters of provenance are certainly important to us in studying any material culture, but we certainly can't overlook the documentation provided by an object itself. Matters of style, technology, and social custom can speak as powerfully as the documented history of an object, and in the case of the "Boon" rifle, they speak clearly enough to provide us with more information than the history of ownership does.

To be as succinct as possible, I believe that it is generally understood among students of the American longrifle who are familiar with this particular weapon that the piece is exceedingly unlikely to have enjoyed actual ownership by Daniel Boone. That is certainly my opinion.

He continued:

The rifle is a southern Appalachian type, showing in its architecture (shaping of the stock), form of the iron mounts (particularly the trigger guard) and the use of a bone heel plate at the butt a combination of details typical of the mountain areas of northwest Georgia, western South Carolina, and southwestern North Carolina. The style of the stock, most particularly the thickness of the butt and the shaping of the wrist area, indicates a probable date range of 1820-30, and this is reinforced by the style of the rifle's lock.

Citing the tendency of pre-1800 American rifles to show "a good deal more of the Baroque heritage of European gunstock design," Mr. Bivins stated: "stocks were more robustly shaped, and buttplates were significantly wider. Rifles of the pre-Revolutionary period often have a buttplate 2" in width or more." He added, "Every aspect of the style of the 'Boon' rifle clearly points to a later period."

In conclusion Mr. Bivins stated that, while Boone undoubtedly had owned a number of longrifles, "I most emphatically do not believe 'Boons best fren' to be one of them." He added: "It could not have been made earlier than the year of Boone's death, and for that matter I don't believe Boone would have so wrtechedly defaced the stock of a rifle in such a manner. I have never seen any longrifle so treated other than a few that had been decorated by plains Indians. In addition, we have no evidence of a gunmaker by the name of Graham."[71]

There have been attempts to account for the proliferating "Boone" carvings, such as this statement in a 1907 issue of the *Register of the Kentucky Historical Society:* "In his declining years, we are told by a great grand-nephew (who had heard the story from his grandfather, Elijah Bryan), Daniel Boone spent his idle hours carving, with his knife, little souvenirs for his family and friends. On all he would cut the initials or full name." That this story is apocryphal is strongly suggested by the remainder of the paragraph: "He gave to his rifles names, it is said, and one of these is in the Historical Society of Missouri, another in the family of a son-in-law in that State, and still another, carved by his own hand, is in the Kentucky State Historical Society."[72] Or so "it is said."

Another "Boon" rifle is in the Kentucky Military History Museum's own collection, but it is kept in storage, presumably because it is such an obvious fake. Its provenance is unknown beyond the fact that it was donated by a Florida man in 1979. Thus the sole "proof" that it belonged to the famous Kentuckian consists of inscriptions on both sides of the stock. On the right-hand side is carved: "D. Boon. CILLED. BIG / PanTHER. this / GUn. I WAS. 13. YEAR. OLD / in. BUCKS. CO. PA." An inscription on the other side has an altered date. In addition to that suspicious detail are the obviously spurious elements of misspelled name and the telltale "CILLED." That word was probably copied from the "BAR" tree with that spelling (mentioned earlier), which was reproduced as a line drawing in a popular 1939 Boone biography.[73] Still another phony element is a series of notches on the stock.

An unsigned typewritten page in the files of the Kentucky Military History Museum, apparently written by a former curator and headed "BOONE RELICS," cites such multiplying rifles as the one formerly on display by the Wisconsin Historical Society and known as early as 1918. Concluded the writer, "One of these guns may have been Daniel Boone's, but certainly not all, and perhaps none of them were."

Among the *uninscribed* rifles sometimes claimed to have belonged to Boone is one in the Tennessee State Museum in Nashville. Its provenance is known from 1852, at which time it was presented to the Tennessee Historical Society by Dr. J.G.M. Ramsey, a longtime president of the society. It is a French musket of a type supplied to American Revolutionary War soldiers and so "could have been used by Daniel Boone," although the museum has "no information as to the basis for this belief."[74]

As might be expected, in addition to alleged Boone rifles, there are also several inscribed powder horns and other items that supposedly belonged to the frontiersman, both inscribed and not.[75]

For example, mentioned in the "BOONE RELICS" typescript

(cited earlier) are a "watch, Daniel Boone's," that "has no prov-enance or authentication at all," and "a walnut beam from Daniel Boone's cabin" in Mason, Missouri, that "could be a piece of an old railroad tie." Another page of typed notes in the Kentucky Military History Museum files refers to a plaster cast belonging to the Kentucky Historical Society that is "said" to be the one made of Boone's skull when his remains were reinterred in Frankfort, al-though one expert thinks it may be negroid.[76] A somewhat com-parable list could be assembled for Daniel's brother, Squire.[77]

All these items, however, represented little more than interest-ing diversions from our primary investigation, namely the question of authenticity of the "Boon hut" with its "D. BooN" carving, together with some of the better know "Boon(e)" inscriptions, such as "BOoNs bESt FREN" and "D. Boon cilled a bar on tree in the year 1760." Orthography, dates, stylistic considerations—all had pro-vided useful investigative approaches to such inscriptions, par-ticularly when actual examination was impossible or simply unproductive. With the "D. BooN" board and "hut" however, examination and analyses were to prove decisive.

We visited the "hut" on several occasions, taking photographs and regarding with enjoyment the fresh inscriptions made by wags: "D. Boon" traced with a finger in the sand under the rock overhang; "D. BOON 1721" carved on the walkway railing; and "D.B." carved at least twice on the railing, once on a nearby rock, and no doubt elsewhere.

We had wanted to examine the "hut" quite closely, and had made arrangements for doing so with the Daniel Boone National Forest's supervisor, Don Fig. Unfortunately some of our ardor was dampened when we learned vandals had crawled under the protec-tive fence and scattered the boards. Although the "hut" had been reconstructed, a massive search for a missing youth in the area repeatedly delayed our examination.

Nevertheless, through the courtesy of Public Information Of-ficer Charles J. Crail, we were able to inspect the "D. BooN" board at the forest office in Winchester, Kentucky. And although a full laboratory inspection was not possible, we were able to study the board briefly, aided by such techniques as macroscopic observation, oblique lighting, and infrared examination, and we took numerous black-and-white and color photographs for further study.

Ironically, many of the types of examination we had envisioned had already been performed. Distressingly, journalists had gener-ally ignored—or even misrepresented—results of two professional analyses contained in reports in the park office files.

The first is a 1967 memorandum report by R.C. Koeppen, botanist, Wood Identification Research, Division of Wood Quality, United States Forest Products Laboratory. The examination showed that the board was split from a red oak tree and turned up even more important information: "The carving was made after the board was well weathered. Evidence for this is chiefly the sharp edges of some letters especially the 'n,' which would be rounded if the carving had been made in sound wood and then weathered."

This was a significant finding, since it is most unlikely that the famous explorer would have found old, ready-made shingles with which to fashion his hut. In fact, botanist Koeppen wrote that, while he could not positively prove it, it was "the general consensus of our staff members that Daniel Boone did not make the carving." He also stated, "The board certainly appears to be very old but it seems to be weathered too much to have been in such a protected place for about 200 years. It gives every evidence of having been quite moist, if not wet, for considerable periods of time. Even the beetle holes are of the type produced by a group that works in wood of a higher moisture content than do the ordinary powder post beetles."[78] In other words, the laboratory examination not only cast extreme doubt on Boone's having done the carving, but it also fully sup-ported other evidence that local schoolboys had actually fashioned the hut.

In the late 1960s, during the brouhaha over discovery of the hut, Powell County resident Henry Catron admitted he had made what was essentially a boy's rustic playhouse about 1935 from wood found in the area.[79] Some journalists and forest employees attempt-ed to cast doubt on Henry Catron's claim, made after he recognized the hut from a television news account and confirmed by a trip to the site.[80] His brother, Hugh, was even quoted as saying Henry must have been mistaken. Interviewed by us, however, Hugh Catron said that, while he did not recall helping them, his brothers Henry and Troy (now deceased) had constructed the hut. "It wasn't made by Boone," he assured us.[81]

Troy Catron, Jr., confirmed Hugh Catron's statement. He said his father had told him that they (Henry and Troy) had built the hut with boards from an old barn that had stood farther down in the hollow (known then as "Catron Hollow," now Martin's Fork).[82]

But even when he was admitting to have fashioned the hut, Henry Catron had disclaimed any knowledge of the "D. BooN" board. As it turns out, that inscription was made by one of the neighborhood boys of a younger generation. The youthful carver was *not* Eugene Peck as had been erroneously claimed in a newspaper article.[83]

However, Eugene Peck told us he believes he knows who did the carving. Peck stated that about 1954, when he lived on Red River, he visited the hut with some other local youths. One of these was off by himself for a time and then showed up with a board on which "D. BooN" was carved. The inscription "looked fresh," and Peck assumed it had just been done. He said the boy was fond of carving his name on beech trees and had a characteristic method of carving: He would mark the letters first with spaced holes, made by gouging and twisting with the point of his pocket knife; then he would connect the "dots" with a gouged line in just the fashion used for the "Boon hut" board.[84] Hugh Catron independently named the same youth, saying he had been told this and had reason to believe it was true.[85]

We mentioned two studies. The second resulted from an inspection of the hut and rock shelter by Martha A. Rolingson, then acting director of the University of Kentucky's Museum of Anthropology. She determined that wooden troughs and paddles, an iron kettle, and other items were "likely to be the remains from a niter mining operation, either in the 1805-1814 period or during the War Between the States." She believed the hut dated from after the niter mining period. As she wrote: "If the hut were constructed by Boone and already in the shelter when the niter mining began, it would probably have been re-used and damaged by the later activities. The low area where the hut is placed could have been dug out by the niter miners processing the sands of the shelter floor."[86]

Quite obviously, our investigation and the previous studies are mutually supportive, and together warrant this conclusion: The so-called "Boon hut" was made, not by Daniel Boone in the eighteenth century, but by the Catron boys about 1935, and the phony "D. BooN" inscription was the product of a schoolboy's pocketknife about 1954.

We are suspicious of Boone inscriptions per se. The notion that Boone was "like modern day kilroys"[87] not only demeans the quiet dignity of the pioneer, hunter, soldier, and surveyor, but is simply contrary to the evidence.[88] Much of the fakery seems intended to foster the popular image of a mighty hunter and Indian fighter—a scarcely literate one, to be sure—rather than, say, that of a surveyor or magistrate. Fortunately for us, hoaxers often exaggerate Boone's lack of education or at least render it inaccurately. Not only was his spelling, as Charles Hamilton said, remarkably consistent; it was also generally a sensible phonetic rendering of his Southern Appalachian speech. For example, Boone wrote "sarvent" for "servant" and "clark" for "clerk."[89]

The bogus carvings often strain credulity to the breaking point. One has to wonder, Why would Boone find it so remarkable to have "cilled a bar on tree" in 1760 when even two decades later the account books for a store he operated routinely gave credit for bear skins? (A single fur traders' consignment included, in addition to 1,790 deerskins and 5 black fox pelts, 729 bearskins.)[90] Or why—given that Boone had sought the shelter of a great cliff overhang but had nevertheless decided to assemble therein a juvenile "hut" scarcely big enough to crawl into—would he literally "hang out a shingle" bearing his misspelled name? Again, why would a soldier deface his rifle with carvings—"BOoNs bESt FREN, a childish picture of an Indian holding an upraised tomahawk, and fifteen notches—when he did not spell his name that way, apparently had a different appellation for his favorite firearm, and could be certain of having killed only a single Indian in his entire life (as he told his son, Nathan)?[91]

To answer these questions with even a modicum of common sense is to do little harm to the memory of Daniel Boone. To the contrary, it is to restore to him a measure of the dignity he deserves—dignity sapped by wags, forgers, credulous biographers, Hollywood filmmakers, well-meaning preservers of Americana, and promoters of tourism.

We are pleased to report that just before our original findings were published in the *Filson Club History Quarterly,* Daniel Boone National Forest officials conceded that the "Boon hut" was a schoolboys' playhouse as we had determined. Subsequently, in 1990, the Kentucky Historical Society displayed an exhibit on Daniel Boone which cast doubt on the various fake inscriptions—including

"BOoNs bESt FREN." Boone would have been pleased. Honest and fair-dealing in his relationships, he could say, in a letter to his sister-in-law after his wife's death, that while he had little formal religion, "I Beleve God neve[r] made a man of my pri[n]sepel to be Lost."[92]

Recommended Works

Cescinsky, Herbert. *The Gentle Art of Faking Furniture*. 1931; reprinted New York: Dover, 1967. Specialized treatise on how antique furniture is faked and how the fakery is detected; 292 plates.

Gilbert, Anne. *How to Be an Antiques Detective*. New York: Grosset and Dunlap, 1978. Overview of antique sleuthing: How to identify and date antiques and to spot fakes; features case histories involving art, furniture, glassware, hardware, silver, textiles, etc.

Hamblin, Dora Jane. *Pots and Robbers*. New York: Simon and Schuster, 1970. Interesting look at Italian archaeologists, *tombaroli* (grave robbers), and forgers—all of whose lives are concerned with Etruscan, Greek, and Roman artifacts. Illustrated.

Katz, Herbert and Marjorie. *Museum Adventures: An Introduction to Discovery*. New York: Coward-McCann, 1969. Exploration of selected large and small museums, and their varied collections, across the United States. Part I features history museums.

Klamkin, Marian and Charles. *Investing in Antiques and Popular Collectibles for Pleasure and Profit*. New York: Funk and Wagnalls, 1975. In addition to main theme, collecting for profit, are sidelights on the pitfalls of reproductions and forgeries.

Mills, John FitzMaurice. *Treasure Keepers*. New York: Doubleday, 1973. Entertaining and informative look at the various aspects of caring for the world's treasured artifacts, including conservation, restoration, investigation, and display.

Panati, Charles. *The Brower's Book of Beginnings: Origin of Everything under (and Including) the Sun*. Boston: Houghton Mifflin, 1984. Compendium on the origins of common objects, customs, etc. Not intended to replace more scholarly, specialized works.

_____. *Extraordinary Origins of Everyday Things*. New York: Harper and Row, 1987. Another compendium of origins of common things ranging from acetate to zipper.

Treasures of America and Where to Find Them. Pleasantville, N.Y.: Reader's Digest Association, 1974. Region-by-region guide, with maps and color photographs, to museums as well as historic and architectural sites.

7 _____ *Suspect Documents*

Lincoln's Bixby Letter

However true the old saw that imitation is the sincerest flattery, something more is usually at stake when it becomes blatant forgery—resentment and greed perhaps, as prompted the spurious letter by the king's bastard son in *Lear*.[1] Shakespeare would himself be victimized by the crime, becoming probably its greatest target. As the late Curtis D. MacDougall, author of *Hoaxes*, wrote: "It is natural that the biggest names should be those most often forged, and the best work that most frequently plagiarized or stolen.[2]

Works bearing Shakespeare's name, but which are now regarded as of doubtful authenticity, appeared in his own lifetime. Certainly a deliberate forgery occurred in 1728 when Lewis Theobald claimed to have discovered a Shakespearean play titled *The Double Falsehood; or the Distrest Lovers*. Actually *The Double Falsehood* was a triple one, but before being exposed as a fake it was performed at Drury Lane and saw two editions.[3]

Additional plays were "discovered" in the 1790s by William Henry Ireland. He had been influenced by a man he had met on a visit to Stratford, John Jordan, the forger of a will of Shakespeare's father. In addition to two plays, Ireland drew up legal contracts and faked various autographed receipts, even a love letter to Anne Hathaway with an enclosed lock of hair.[4] He was exposed by Shakespearean critic Edmund Malone, and he later confessed publicly.[5]

Among the documents deliberately intended to falsify history are the so-called Donation of Constantine and the False Decretals. The former—a blatant forgery believed produced at Rome in the eighth century—granted Roman Pontiffs spiritual authority within Christendom, as well as temporal supremacy over Rome, Italy, and the Italian provinces. Supposedly the "Donation" (of the emperor's crown, Lateran Palace, and provinces of the Italian peninsula) was in gratitude for Constantine's alleged miraculous recovery from leprosy and his conversion to Christianity.

The false Decretals (papal decrees) appeared in the tenth century, having been devised to establish the antiquity of papal authority. The forger slyly incorporated some genuine elements into the epistles, thereby helping to mask the spurious ones.

Both the Donation and the False Decretals survived detection for centuries. Even after being suspected, the latter withstood decisive rejection until the third quarter of the sixteenth century, and the Donation's defenders were not silenced until the close of the eighteenth century.[6] In the meantime, according to hoax authority MacDougall: "As Christianity spread, the emulators of the authors of the False Decretals and the Donation of Constantine became legion. To give greater weight to their own essays and homilies, churchmen thought nothing of attaching the names of holy fathers whose authority was recognized. Erasmus was known to have complained that he possessed not a single work of the fathers upon the genuineness of which he could depend."[7]

Secular examples are likewise legion. Among the "discoveries" inflicted on the historical community are a letter to Columbus from Queen Isabella, who offered to pawn her jewels to finance the explorer's expedition. It is, of course, dated 1492, but—less appropriately—is written in modern Spanish. It accompanies another forged treasure, Columbus's own "Secrete Log Booke," a hilarious creation, complete with glued-on seashells and bits of kelp.[8]

Other audacious historical forgeries include a bullet-riddled note by General Custer, appealing for help from the Little Big Horn;[9] a death warrant for a Salem witch, carrying the signatures of Cotton Mather, John Winthrop, and other historical personages;[10] and the "original draft" of the Declaration of Independence—supposedly in Jefferson's handwriting but penned by the infamous Joseph Cosey.[11]

Cosey also forged the writings of Benjamin Franklin and other notables, but he specialized in Abraham Lincoln letters and legal briefs. Many of these still lie in wait for the unsuspecting researcher.[12] The Great Emancipator has been a frequent subject of the forger's art,[13] and "manufactured Lincoln letters have found their way even into printed compilations of his papers."[14]

Perhaps America's most notorious autograph forger was Robert

Spring. Born in England in 1813, Spring came to America as a young man and took up the trade of bookseller in Philadelphia. He soon discovered that adding the signature of George Washington to a book's title page improved its salability, and thus his nefarious career was launched. Fake Washingtons were a specialty, as Charles Hamilton notes: "Using a goose quill and his own special mixture of 'antiquated' ink, he practiced constantly to capture the spirit and verve of Washington's handwriting. He was extremely successful. One of his Washington forgeries was ostentatiously displayed in Independence Hall."15

Notable twentieth-century purveyors of historical fakes are Konrad Kujau, who penned the multi-volume "Hitler Diaries," and Mark Hofmann, who forged Mormon-related papers and other historic documents, including a Daniel Boone letter, then turned to bombing murders in an attempt to thwart exposure.

Not only the great have been targeted, however. Occasionally forgers and hoaxers turned their talents to discovering important works that were allegedly produced by unknown, or previously unknown, writers. Often-cited examples are the verses allegedly written by a medieval monk named Rowley, which were actually forgeries by the youthful poet Thomas Chatterton, and Gaelic epics attributed to a Homeric figure called Ossian, which were actually penned by James MacPherson.16 Another instance would be the Rev. R.S. Hawker's imitative folk ballad, "Song of the Westward Men." Although it was apparently not intended to deceive, it nevertheless found its way into an anthology of ancient Scottish ballads whose editor asserted, "They are, indeed, not such compositions as a literary impostor would think it worthwhile to produce."17

The bogus ballad case should serve to warn against the assumption—all too often expressed—that some autograph or relatively inexpensive letter or document "would not be worth enough to forge." There are other incentives for forgery and hoaxes than pecuniary ones. For example, Vermeer forger Van Meegeren (mentioned in the previous chapter) explained that his motive was revenge against the art critics who had rejected his early paintings.18

Moreover—again as the example of the ballad illustrates—not all works that are inauthentic are deliberate fakes. A case in point would be an old document brought to me by a dealer in Americana. It bore genuine signs of age, and among the names listed in two columns with a quill pen was "David Crockett." The document was dated, although one digit was uncertain, but it bore no place name or heading that suggested its purpose. Moreover, the possibility of handwriting comparison was ruled out since the entire roster was in a clerk's hand. In short, the dealer wished to know whether the name on the authentic document was that of the famous Tennessean.

Selecting several of the more unusual names and matching them against federal census records demonstrated that the document originated from the county in Tennessee where lived *the* Davy Crockett. Unfortunately, there were *three* of that name, but evidence from the date (from the two possible interpretations of it) rendered it unlikely to have been the name of the later hero of the Alamo.

Another category of nonforgery fakes was exemplified by a supposed holographic draft of the literary masterpiece, the Gettysburg Address. Its owners, a rural family, had been in turn to an archivist, a professional handwriting expert, and a conservationist—all of whom had apparently expressed varying degrees of puzzlement—until university archival librarians suggested it be shown to me. It was a reproduction, printed on imitation parchment, such as is sold in tourist shops in the nation's capital.

A further example of the same category was an apparent clerical copy of "General Order No. 9," relating to the surrender of the confederacy and bearing the signature of General Lee. If authentic it would have been quite valuable, but held to the light, its prominent watermark failed to show translucency, and magnification revealed the ultra-fine screen-pattern of dots that demonstrated the entire document—including the back with its stains and other markings—was a halftone reproduction.[19]

Some other questioned documents—another Lee, a few early land grants, and a Tennyson autograph—will help suggest the range of problems that can be encountered by the historical investigator and some of the approaches he or she might take to resolve them.

The first was a carte de visite photo of the rebel leader, signed in ink, "R E Lee / *Genl.*" A collector had purchased it at a price that was suspiciously—or disarmingly?—low. Magnification showed tremors in the pen strokes that were indicative of a slowly drawn forgery, but were also somewhat similar to the shakiness that can result from age.[20] However, comparison with genuine Lee signatures from the last years of his life which were smoothly penned, coupled with tests which showed the ink was inconsistent with inks of the period, revealed the autograph was a forgery.

The procedure with the land grants that were encountered—which were partially printed and filled in on parchment, and bearing affixed seals—was first to determine their genuineness. A familiarity with such documents and with genuine signs of age facilitated that task based on visual inspection. It remained to determine whether the signatures were those of presidents Madison, Van Buren, and others, or whether they were proxy signatures by secretaries. Comparison of each with several known standards (facsimiles are satisfactory for such limited purposes) demonstrated which were actually signed by the presidents.

A Monroe grant invited extra scrutiny. The name written at the top was an obvious alteration which consisted of the original *printed* name having been scraped away with an ink-eraser knife and "James Monroe" being penned over that roughened area. An examination, however, showed that the signature at the bottom was the president's own, down with a quill. The date of the document, in the first days of Monroe's term, provided an explanation for the alteration: the president's own forms had not yet been printed, and the name of his predecessor was being scratched off some old forms that were being pressed into service.

The Tennyson autograph presented several interesting features. It was framed with an engraved portrait of the poet and first appeared to be a "cut signature" (one clipped from a letter or other document). However, when it was removed it was found to be a larger slip of paper bearing a penned notation. Where the paper had been mounted behind a cutout rectangle in the mat, a corresponding rectangle of yellowing had resulted; this provided a sign of age (although not necessarily an indication of authenticity). The paper was a calendared, machine-made variety that was correct for the time period. The ink appeared corrosive, indicative of an iron-gallotannate ink acting over time, and that was confirmed by testing an insignificant sample removed from the inscription. This read, "Written in the Isle of Wight 5th April 1866/WHB." Investigation readily showed that Tennyson was at that place during that time period, and suggested a possible candidate for the initials: William Henry Brookfield, a friend and neighbor of the then poet laureate.[21]

While the foregoing is not intended as a complete manual of authentication, it points to approaches that should prove helpful in many cases, and should stimulate thinking in others. Recall also some of the methods employed in earlier chapters.

Finally, something should be said about provenance (briefly mentioned in the previous chapter). It is always desirable to learn the true provenance (or chain of ownership) of a work.[22] Still, as Roy L. Davids says regarding questions of authenticity, "provenance can be important, but it can never be unimpeachable—externals must always be inferior to a thorough examination of the manuscript itself."[23] Worse, provenances can themselves be faked.[24]

Obviously, provenance will hold more interest concerning a sensational work, and the refusal of the possessor of an item to state where and how he obtained it—the infamous case of the "Hitler Diaries" comes to mind—must be interpreted accordingly. Certainly, contradictory stories with regard to provenance (again the "Hitler Diaries" case is an instance) or evidence of faked provenance should prompt the most thorough investigation and examination of a work in question.

With this in mind, we can now turn to an important case that presents many of the problems we have been discussing. It concerns a letter which has proliferating "originals" that are typically copies of a forgery. And there are even claims that Abraham Lincoln did not write the eloquent letter so many have come to admire. Just who did author the letter to Mrs. Bixby?

Among the best known—yet greatly disputed and controversial— of the writings attributed to Abraham Lincoln is the epistle allegedly sent to a Mrs. Bixby at the height of the Civil War. The letter consoles the Boston lady on the reported loss of five sons, all of whom had supposedly died battling for the Union cause. Published widely, the letter reads:

Executive Mansion,
Washington. Nov. 21, 1864.

To Mrs. Bixby, Boston, Mass.

Dear Madam:
I have been shown in the files of the War department a statement of the Adjutant-General of Massachusetts that you are the mother of five sons who have died gloriously on the field of battle. I feel how weak and fruitless must be any word of mine which should attempt to beguile you from the

grief of a loss so overwhelming. But I cannot refrain from tendering you the consolation that may be found in the thanks of the republic they died to save. I pray that our Heavenly Father may assuage the anguish of your bereavement, and leave you only the cherished memory of the loved and lost, and the solemn pride that must be yours to have laid so costly a sacrifice upon the altar of freedom.

Yours very sincerely and respectfully,

A. Lincoln[25]

Although a facsimile of the handwritten letter (Figure 16) was published in the *Complete Works of Abraham Lincoln*, edited by the slain president's former secretaries, John G. Nicolay and John Hay,[26] it is now known that the handwriting was forged. Charles Hamilton, the internationally known authority on autographs who once owned that "original" manuscript, states that is was "retraced, labored, erased and thoroughly unconvincing," adding, "In it, the forger had stumbled badly. The paper was not of the variety used by Lincoln, the ink was modern, the folds were not correct to accommodate envelopes of Lincoln's era and the letter itself had first been drawn in pencil and then traced in ink. Yet this forged missive has been published in facsimile in scores of history books and hung in the parlors of half a million homes." Hamilton states he is offered a Bixby fake as an "original" several times a year.[27]

My own interest in the letter was rekindled not long ago when an antique dealer asked me to examine a document he had acquired. Because it was imprinted with the engraved portrait of Lincoln,[28] I knew—even from a dozen feet away—that it was spurious, but I nevertheless examined it carefully with a strong magnifier. Cheaply printed on cheap paper, it was, of course, merely another example of the proliferating fake—a facsimile of a forgery.

But had there been a genuine letter that provided the text for the forgery, or was even that completely bogus? (Lincoln's fame invited just such fabrications, including the one to a Pennsylvania Dutchman written in German, a language Lincoln could not even read.)[29] Hamilton says of the Bixby epistle: "Nobody knows whether Lincoln really composed this great letter or whether, if he did write it, it was ever mailed."[30]

Nevertheless, in an 1894 essay, "Lincoln as a Writer," Richard Watson Gilder implicitly accepted the authenticity of the letter's text and stated it "may well be associated with the Gettysburg Ad-

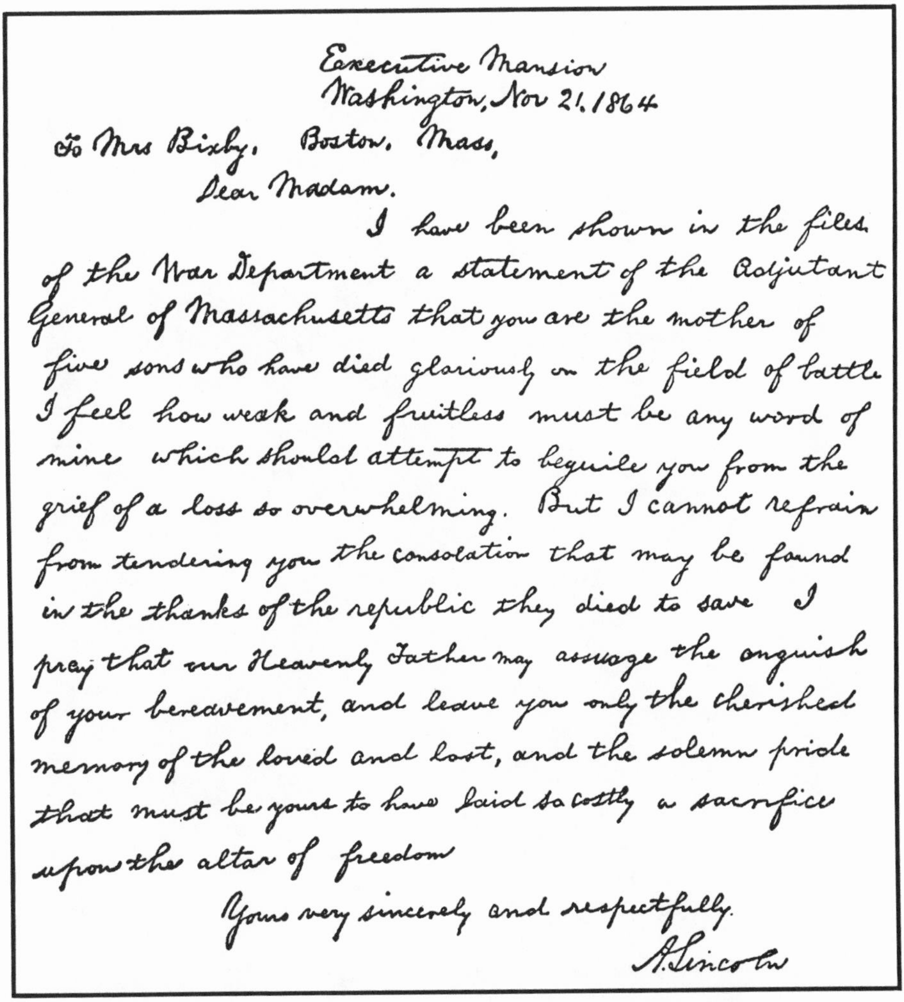

Figure 16. Forged text of Lincoln's letter to the widow Bixby. The original of the letter is now lost.

dress."[31] Another who accepts the genuineness of the text is manuscript dealer Mary A. Benjamin. As she has written, "these words are practically universally accepted as those of Abraham Lincoln. . . . Librarians and experts in the autograph field have for many years accepted the fact that an original Lincoln-Bixby letter existed. The core of the authorities' question is: Was the Bixby letter originally an L.S. [letter signed] or an A.L.S. [autograph letter

Figure 17. Abraham Lincoln with his secretary, John Hay, in a photograph made in 1863. Hay, according to some reports, wrote the famous letter to Mrs. Bixby.

signed]? Was it written in the handwriting of Lincoln at all? Was it even signed by him?"[32] She adds, "the years have kept silence on this enigma, and perhaps it may never be solved."[33]

Not surprisingly, however, there have been dissenters—notably Sherman Day Wakefield, author of two articles and as many pamphlets on the subject. He compared the Bixby text to that of a letter of condolence Lincoln wrote to the daughter of a slain officer, Lt. Col. William McCullough. Stated Wakefield: "Now style is a difficult thing to describe; it is rather something to be felt, and I do not feel that the Bixby letter and the McCullough letter are in the same category." Following that subjective judgment, Wakefield conceded: "Of course the former is written to a stranger and the latter to an old friend, which would, I suppose, make some difference." Yet he must ask, "But why would Lincoln, if he believed in a 'Heavenly Father' fail to give the consolation of religion to a loved friend in his letter of condolence and then extend it to an utter stranger? That is not like Lincoln, and the comparison only serves to throw further doubt on the genuineness of the Bixby letter."[34] Actually, in a letter to the bereaved parents of a slain soldier, a young Colonel Ellsworth, Lincoln did write: "May God give you the consolation which is beyond all earthly power."[35]

More significant to Wakefield is the "fact" that Lincoln's secretary, John Hay (Figure 17), twice confided to others that he had written the Bixby letter. The first source was a Mr. Lucas, who published in 1934 a letter received from a Reverend Jackson, who had heard from Lady Strafford, who had learned from an Ambassador Page, who had been told by John Hay.[36]

The second source, a 1940 autobiography, was only at third hand, but it was couched in secrecy: Supposedly Hay asked that the fact of his authorship be kept secret until his death, and the person he confided in made a similar request of the person he in turn told.[37] As Mary Benjamin comments, "Where there is secrecy on matters which cannot be substantiated by records, suspicion is inevitable."[38] Moreover, both of these accounts contain a similar motif—both were supposedly elicited by the seeing of framed copies of the letter—which suggests the possibility that the hearsay accounts are merely variant folktales.

In any event, Lincoln historian William E. Barton stated, "I have made diligent inquiry of the family of John Hay, and . . . they, who ought to know of this if anyone knows, profess to have no knowledge that supports such a claim."[39] In addition, the accounts are effectively challenged by a letter written by Hay on January 19, 1904, that states, "The letter of Mr. Lincoln to Mrs. Bixby is genuine, is printed in our edition of his Works, and had been frequently republished; but the engraved copy of Mr. Lincoln's alleged manuscript, which is extensively sold is, in my opinion, a very ingenious forgery."[40]

There should be no doubt that a letter addressed to Mrs. Bixby was actually sent from the Lincoln White House. First of all, there really was a Mrs. Lydia (Parker) Bixby (ca. 1801-1878) who lived at various addresses in Boston where she was alternately described as "nurse" and "widow." She indeed had five sons who fought for the Union.[41]

Actually, however, only two died in battle (Charles N. Bixby on May 3, 1863, and Oliver Cromwell Bixby on July 30, 1864). Another son (Henry Cromwell Bixby) was erroneously reported killed at Gettysburg, but he had actually been captured, was later paroled, and finally received an honorable discharge. Mrs. Bixby's other two sons (Edward and George May) deserted to the enemy. Edward later expatriated himself, but George sought exile in Cuba where his brothers and sisters last heard from him in 1879.[42]

Precisely how the misunderstanding arose—that five of Mrs. Bixby's sons had been killed—is not known, but the result is reflected in the title of the definitive work on the subject by Barton, *A Beautiful Blunder.* He cites a letter written to the governor of Massachusetts by Adjutant-General Schouler which stated, in part, "About ten days ago Mrs. Bixby came to my office and showed me five letters from five company commanders, and each letter informed the poor woman of the death of one of her sons. Her last remaining son was recently killed in the fight on the Weldon railroad."[43] Whether Schouler misunderstood the details, Mrs. Bixby misrepresented the facts, or there is still some other explanation is unknown.

Nevertheless, confirming the important fact that President Lincoln had sent the Boston widow the now-famous letter are the November 25, 1864, issues of the Boston *Transcript* and *Traveller,* in which the text first appeared. This was the day after Adjutant-General Schouler delivered the letter to Mrs. Bixby.[44]

Whether Lincoln had also composed the letter was a question I addressed in a lengthy study of the text. As Wakefield said, style is

Table 1. A Comparison of Lincoln Phraseology (the numbers in parentheses refer to the volume and page in Nicolay and Hay's *Complete Works*).

Gettysburg Address	*Other Lincoln Writings*
It is altogether fitting and proper	it is altogether befitting (6: 139); it is most proper (6: 134); it has seemed to me fit and proper (9: 152)
. . . the unfinished work which they who fought here have thus far so nobly advanced	the blood they have so nobly shed (11: 125); to advance the great cause (6: 130)
that government of the people, by the people, for the people, shall not perish from the earth.	a government of the people by the same people (6: 304); will endure forever (5: 49).

difficult to describe, but there are modern techniques that facilitate an objective study. Unfortunately, these usually involve a statistical tabulation of identifiable writing habits—for example, sentences beginning with "The," passive negative constructions, or the like[45]—and the length of the Bixby letter's text (only 130 words between the salutation and closing) was less than desirable for such an analysis. Yet it was possible to look for distinctive words and phrases, comparable expressions of thought, similar rhythms, and the like—forms that might then be exhibited in side-by-side comparison, in the manner of demonstrating similarity of handwriting characteristics or fingerprint patterns.[46]

To see how such an approach might work, we can look at its application in an example in which Lincoln's authorship is unquestioned, the Gettysburg Address, of which we have Lincoln's actual drafts in his own handwriting.[47] The accompanying chart (Table 1) compares excerpts from the famous speech with specimens of Lincoln's phraseology from his other writings. As can be seen, the excerpts are sufficiently distinctive to have evidential value and are quite similar.

Of course someone with the intelligence, vocabulary, and creativity of a Lincoln may be expected to employ phrases that are unique. One looks in vain, for example, for another use by Lincoln of "Fourscore and seven years ago. . . ." The closest match would seem to be the opening words of his 1852 "Eulogy on Henry Clay": "On the fourth day of July, 1776, the people . . . " (2:155). Yet the historical referent is the same, as is its function as the opening of an oration. And the difference can be attributed to the overall height-

Table 2. A Comparison of the Bixby Text with Lincoln Writing.

Bixby Letter	*Lincoln Writings*
Dear Madam:	My Dear Madam (10: 253)
I have been shown in the files of the War Department a statement of the Adjutant-General of Massachusetts that you are the mother of five sons	I see your despatch to the Secretary of War (11: 50); There have recently reached the War Department, and thence been laid before me, from Missouri, three communications (9: 186)
Who have died gloriously on the field of battle.	who . . . so gallantly periled their lives in battling with the enemy (10: 212); their devotion to our glorious cause (11: 125)
I feel how weak and fruitless must be any words of mine	too weak (1: 42); fruitless every attempt (1: 43); what so humble an individual as myself chose to say (5: 36);
which should attempt to beguile you from the grief	which might divert your mind (1: 183); no intrusion upon the sacredness of your sorrow (6: 288)
of a loss so overwhelming.	of a work so vast (9: 215); of a citizen so venerable(10: 276); support so unanimously given (10: 101)
But I cannot refrain from tendering to you the consolation that may be found in the thanks of the Republic they died to save.	I tender to you . . . the thanks of the nation (10: 213); the nation's sympathy (7: 14); those who here gave their lives that that nation might live (9: 209-10).

ening of the language in the Gettysburg speech, no doubt influenced by Lincoln's intuitive evocation of the style of the King James Bible.

Turning now to the questioned text, the Bixby letter, we again find comparable wording in Lincoln's letters and speeches (the Bixby letter having features of both) as shown in Table 2.

Some traits were especially noteworthy, such as Lincoln's frequent use of the verb *to tender.* Just as the Bixby letter uses "tendering," Lincoln—in a few pages of his writings from December 24, 1860, to February 8, 1861[48]—employed the following: "Tender you my sincere thanks," "that it was tendered you," "so kindly tendered," "cordially tendered to him," "tendering me," "so generously tendered," "cordially tendered me," "tendered this invitation," and "the tendered honor."

Table 2 (Continued)

I pray that our heavenly Father may assuage	I pray God (10: 170); prayers to our Father in Heaven (10: 216); invoke the influence of his Holy Spirit to subdue (9: 33); more sorrow assuaged (1: 208)
the anguish of your bereavement,	the sad bereavement you mention (10: 330); the depths of afflication (5: 255)
and leave you only the cherished memory	its beloved history and cherished memories (7: 273)
of the loved and lost	from these honored dead (9: 210); The death-scenes of those we love (1: 186); loved ones lost (1: 291)
and the solemn pride that must be yours	may justly pride themselves (6: 329); solemn awe (1: 209); a matter of honor and pride (1: 266)
to have laid so costly a sacrifice upon the altar of freedom.	the blood they have so nobly shed (11: 125); the temple of liberty (1: 49); sacrifice unceasingly upon its altars (1: 43).
Yours very sincerely and respectfully,	Yours very truly (10: 142); Very respectfully (6: 272),
A. Lincoln	A. Lincoln (6: 288).

The use of alliteration for rhetorical effect (Lincoln wrote some competent verse) is another evidential feature. In the Bixby letter, such alliterative forms as "beguile you from the grief, "assuage the anguish," and "loved and lost" are matched by instances from known writings of Lincoln, as "for weal or for woe" (8: 217), "sacredness of your sorrow" (6: 288), "scorned and scouted" (2: 167), "blows and bloodshed" (2: 239), "lamp of liberty" (3: 52), and "loved ones lost" (1: 291).

Following my own study, I asked Professor Jean Pival, a specialist in English linguistics and rhetoric,[49] to compare the Bixby text with the writings of both Lincoln and Hay.[50] Having assisted me in solving other literary cases,[51] Professor Pival readily agreed. Upon completion of her analysis of the two men's styles, she wrote:

There is more than a generational difference in their syntax and vocabulary; it is a well-known fact that Lincoln's style was strongly influenced by his intensive reading of Elizabethan literature, particularly Shakespeare and the King James version of the Bible. Consequently, he integrated

Elizabethan syntactical structures which, in all probability, had disappeared even in the frontier of his youth. Certainly they were supplanted by more modern usages in the speech and writings of formally educated Easterners. Although both Lincoln and Hay grew up in Indiana, Hay went to the east where he attended and graduated from Brown University. True, Hay studied law in Illinois for a short time after his graduation, but Lincoln was a certified lawyer who actively practiced law for over twenty years. Legal usages and formal argument structures abound even in his personal letters, while Hay's writings show little or no influence of such background. Whereas Hay's personal writings are full of the slang contemporary to his youth, Lincoln's letters are more formal in character—even old-fashioned. For instance, Lincoln's writings (particularly his earlier ones) are rampant with Elizabethan conditionals (conditionals without a conditional conjunction [if] and with the subjective verb form):

Examples: "should she be destined . . ."
"But should I be mistaken in this . . ."
"in case my mind *were* not exactly right . . ."

Even when he used conditional conjunctions, he tended to pair them with "shall," "should," "be," or "were":

Examples: "When they shall be safe . . ."
"if I shall determine . . ."
"lest you should think . . ."
"that the delegates all be instructed . . ."
"that the military were . . ."

I found none of these usages in the Hay letters I examined.

Lincoln preferred "shall" and "should" over "will" and "would" throughout all his writings; Hay almost always used the latter. This fact is significant to the Bixby letter in the phrase "which should attempt to beguile you." Hay, even if trying to emulate Lincoln's style, would almost certainly have used "would."

She continued:

One striking contrast in the stylistic options of the two men was in their choice of verb phrases; Hay's writing exhibits an unusually high frequency of the perfect aspect, i.e. *have shown* (his April 10,1863, letter to Lincoln is the most glaring). Lincoln used this aspect sparingly and only when no other aspect would work, preferring instead to use past tense or progressive aspect, i.e. *is going*. Similarly, Hay's use of passive far exceeds Lincoln's who preferred active voice (except when avoiding "I" as the subject in passages dealing with his accomplishments—as in a Thanksgiving Proclamation). Note that the Bixby letter uses the perfect aspect only once as a main verb and a passive only twice: in the first sentence to avoid unnecessary identity of the person who showed him the files, and to enhance the emphasis the writer wished to place on the "thanks of the republic."

I can add little to your excellent analysis of the vocabulary except to point out that Lincoln's use of "beguile" is in the Elizabethan sense of *diverting*. Hay's meaning in his letter to Mrs. R., March 19, 1861, is closer to the contemporary sense: "to charm or entice."

Lincoln's use of "tender" in the other writings you mentioned is the same as in the Bixby letter—the legal meaning of "offer."

Also, the metaphor of "laid so costly a sacrifice on the altar of freedom" is consistent with coined metaphors found in other Lincoln letters; i.e., "might also be the nest in which forty other troublesome questions would be hatched." Hay would more likely have used a literary quotation.

Professor Pival ended by stating:

Despite the difficulty of doing a close analysis of such a short piece of writing, my conclusion is that Lincoln wrote the letter himself. There is too much stylistic evidence to believe otherwise.[52]

Thus the stylistic comparison confirms what is already demonstrated by the documentary record and other historical indications. The cumulative evidence clearly restores the pen to the great president's hand and reveals the Bixby letter as his own.

Recommended Works

Hamilton, Charles. *Great Forgers and Famous Fakes: The Manuscript Forgers of America and How they Duped the Experts.* New York: Crown, 1980. Essential text for anyone interested in historic forgeries, providing an entertaining look at the lives of forgers; nicely illustrated, with chapter on detecting forgeries.

Morton, A.Q. *Literary Detection: How to Prove Authorship and Fraud in Literature and Documents.* New York: Scribner's, 1978. Presentation of "stylometric analysis," a means of identifying authorship on the basis of certain stylistic elements.

Nickell, Joe. *Pen, Ink, and Evidence.* Lexington, Ky.: University Press of Kentucky, 1990. Nuts-and-bolts approach to document study, in five parts: pens, ink, paper, writing, examining; profusely illustrated from author's collection.

Osborn, Albert S. *Questioned Documents.* 2d ed. Montclair, N.J.: Patterson Smith, 1978. Classic text recommended as much for its treatment of the basics of document examination as for its technical information.

Cooke's "Missing" Edition

In addition to questioned writings, another category of document-related problems the historical investigator frequently encounters is that of lost texts. By *text* is meant the wording or words of something written or printed or even voice-recorded. Texts of one kind or another represent the essential foundation upon which knowledge of the past is constructed.

A text may be "lost" in any of numerous ways. It may be destroyed, as by fire, or be hidden in some manner, or rendered unintelligible, faded, or otherwise difficult to read by the passage of time. The restoration of texts involves a variety of approaches ranging from the mere enhancement of dim writing to attempts to reconstruct a text (or at best the data it contained) completely from alternate sources.

Consider the case of Lord Byron's memoirs. Aware of its scandalous contents, and learning of the poet's death in Greece, a group of his friends and family representatives convened at the London home of John Murray, owner of the manuscript. With the majority in agreement and over the protests of Byron's friend, Thomas Moore, the papers were tossed into the fire. Although copies were rumored to exist, none has ever surfaced. Yet Byron scholars believe that the information in the memoir has now largely been reconstructed from other sources, such as the poet's journal (subsequently published by Moore in his biography of Byron) and his many letters.[1]

Similar reconstructive efforts were initiated for some old Kentucky records that are of considerable interest to genealogists. They are the marriage records of Montgomery County, which perished in 1863 when the courthouse was torched by Confederate cavalry.

Beginning by indexing the private records of two early ministers, the author's friend, Hazel Mason Boyd, added such additional proof of marriages as could be gleaned, for example, from Bible records, post-fire deeds and wills, tombstone inscriptions, and family genealogical papers. Alphabetized, cross-indexed, and documented, a bookful of the marriages was published in 1961[2]—a small monument to perseverance.

Inspired by such work, the author constructed a partial settlement list for the portion of eastern Kentucky that later became Morgan County. The records needed for the purpose—deeds, surveys, tax lists, and the like—were lost when the parent county's log courthouse burned in 1808.[3]

However, it became possible to employ *negative* evidence to provide the essential data. As it happened, there had been virtually a mass migration into the county from a small area to the west, as intermarried families had sought the cheap, neglected eastern hill country of "Kentucky's last frontier." Tax lists from the county of origin were extant from the end of the eighteenth century, making it possible to track certain names—names identified by their appearance in post-1808 Floyd records—year by year. When they were eventually dropped from the tax rolls, a probable date of emigration was indicated.[4]

Quite a different challenge for investigators was presented by several of Charles Dickens's letters. In contrast to many that had been destroyed by his family, some simply had offending passages inked out. Infrared photography, however, enabled Dickens scholars to read the obliterated portions, which contained references to "Nelly" and thus confirmed what had long been rumored: For the last dozen years of his life, Dickens had kept a mistress named Ellen Ternan, a young woman the same age as his younger daughter.[5]

Infrared photography has also been used to read charred documents[6] and to restore the original text of palimpsests (erased and written-over parchment manuscripts).[7] Ultraviolet light may also work in the latter case,[8] and it is useful for many other decipherment problems: enhancing old, faded inks;[9] disclosing the use of secret inks;[10] and revealing alterations of writing.[11] (See Figures 18 and 19.)

Many ancient texts have been destroyed or otherwise lost over time, leaving only copies that exist in varying degrees of accuracy. For example, there are more than eighty manuscripts of portions of

Figure 18. Portable ultraviolet lights (suitable for genealogists to take to the courthouse) are available for use in enhancing dim writing, detecting altera- tions, and so forth.

Geoffrey Chaucer's great fourteenth-century classic, *Canterbury Tales*. Yet none is original (that is, from Chaucer's pen), and none quite agrees with any other owing to copying and recopying. As Richard Altick explains in his *The Scholar Adventurers:*

What the student of a medieval text must do, therefore—and what Manly and Rickert did in the case of the *Canterbury Tales*—is to study every known manuscript of the work and compare its set of variants with that found in every other one. By laboriously classifying the manuscripts according to the position, number, and nature of the variants, he can in time erect a

Figure 19. Although not always successful, the enhancement of faded ink by ultraviolet light, as shown here, is often dramatic. (Photos by Robert H. van Outer.)

Stammbaum—a family tree of manuscripts, which shows how Manuscript Z was derived from Manuscript Y, which in turn was copied from Manuscript X; and Manuscript X may have been a fourth-generation descendant of Manuscript Q, from which, by an independent line of descent, Manuscripts R, S, and T, which have a quite different set of variants, were successively copied. The eventual result of all this work is the pushing of the text back through the centuries to the manuscript that seems to have been the ultimate ancestor of all the different branches of the family, as is shown by the fact that it has fewer of the errors that characterize the rest as a result of successive recopying. This version, the Cain of the line if not the

Adam, is called (relatively) "pure text." While it may not represent exactly what the author himself wrote, it is the closest the scholar can come to it in lack of the author's own manuscript.[12]

The early printed texts of Shakespeare's plays contain numerous garbled phrases to challenge textual scholars. But they have proven worthy of the task, applying several sophisticated methods to it: studying both Elizabethan handwriting and pronunciation (some think the early printers had the manuscripts read aloud for typesetting), as well as other factors. The result is that the text of modern editions of the Bard's works has been rendered much less corrupt.[13]

An example of just how the misreading of handwriting can occur comes from an instance the author encountered. The published text of an eighteenth-century document concerning a land claim contained the phrase, "the Cardinal points of the Camp aforesaid,"[14] which is meaningless. Reference to the original document[15] showed that the last two words had derived from what resembled "Camp afs." Actually, however, that was a single word, with an "a" for an "o" and the "f" an old-fashioned "long s"; thus the correct phrase was "the Cardinal points of the *Compass*"—i.e., north, south, east, and west.

Just as time has rendered the quaint "long s" confusing to most people, the ancient Egyptian writings had become so removed from modern scholars that they were completely unintelligible. Then came the key in the form of a black basalt slab, the celebrated Rosetta Stone, secured by the British in 1801. Its inscription (promoting the policies of boy-King Ptolemy V in 196 B.C.) was thrice given: once each in hieroglyphics, demotic script, and Greek. Since the latter was known, Egyptologists were enabled to unlock the secrets of hieroglyphics and eventually to translate the ancient texts routinely.[16]

In the case of the even more ancient cuneiform ("wedge-shaped") writing of the Sumerians, Assyrians, and Babylonians, it was proper names and titles at the beginning of inscriptions that provided initial keys for decipherment. They, in turn, permitted certain sound values to be determined, and—eventually—paleographers were able to interpret the various cuneiform languages, thus rescuing them from the domain of the lost.[17]

A more recent decipherment problem was presented by the

diary of Samuel Pepys (1633-1703), which appeared to be written in some sort of code. Eventually Lord Granville—onetime British secretary of state for foreign affairs, who thus had a rudimentary knowledge of secret writing—was able to translate a few pages. Then, employing a partial key Lord Granville provided, a student at St. John's College named John Smith spent three years of hard work completing the decipherment. Thus were salvaged Pepys's invaluable observations about life in post-Restoration London. Ironically, after Smith's death it was discovered that Pepys had simply employed a particular system of shorthand—published and available to Smith, had he known to look, at the very library where he labored.[18]

Likewise retrieved—in this case rescued from the limbo of a millennium—were previously unknown documents now referred to as the Dead Sea Scrolls. They have led to the reassessment of certain Old Testament problems and have shed light on Christianity's antecedents. They were accidentally discovered in a cave in 1947 by a Bedouin youth who, according to one version of the story, was searching for a lost sheep. Instead, he found lost sheepskins— parchment scrolls stored in pottery jars and representing "the greatest manuscript discovery of modern times."[19]

Then there is the case of the "lost" papers of James Boswell (1740-1795), biographer of Samuel Johnson. Rumored destroyed, they had actually been passed down through five generations of descendants. They were discovered over several years in a series of caches: stored in an "ebony cabinet" (actually a black-oak escritoire), stuffed in a unused croquet box, and stashed in a stable loft— all at Malahide Castle, near Dublin; and they were also found crammed in metal boxes, great wooden chests, and a seed-bean sack—located in a rambling, Scottish country mansion known as Fettercairn House. Reunited after a century and a half, they were acquired by Yale University and made available to literary specialists to glean information about Johnson, Boswell, and their contemporaries.[20]

On an even grander scale is an entire *edition* of an important American book that has supposedly been lost since colonial times. At least that is a conclusion that has been drawn from the work's textual history. It represents an intriguing story which we now examine.

According to Edward H. Cohen, "In all of colonial American literature there is no problem so perplexing as that of the textual history of the *Sot-weed Factor.*"[21] This textual problem concerns a possibly "lost" second edition of Ebenezer Cooke's hudibrastic satire, the first edition of which was published in London in 1708.[22]

A "sot-weed factor" can be defined as a tobacco merchant, and Cook's satire presents a contemptuous view of American planters and life in the tobacco-producing colonies. Little is known about Cooke (or Cook), but he was probably born in 1665 or 1667 in England, probably the son of Andrew and Anne (Bowyer) Cooke who had married the year before. From a reference in his poem it has been conjectured that he may have attended Cambridge. The poem represents him as an Englishman who visited America, and in 1694 a person of that name, a freeman of St. Mary's City, did sign a petition against moving the capital of Maryland to Annapolis. After his father's death in 1711, he and his sister Anna inherited land in Maryland known as Cooke's Point. In 1717 they sold their respective shares in the land, at which time Cooke was definitely living in Maryland. From 1720 to 1722 he was a deputy to the receiver-general of the province, and in 1728 he was admitted to legal practice in Prince George's County. In December of that year he published an elegy on the death of Nicholas Lowe signed "E. Cooke. Laureat," a title possibly bestowed by Lord Baltimore. An earlier elegy, "An Elogy on Thomas Bordley," was published in 1726. Other works included *Sotweed Redivivus* (1730), "The History of Colonel Nathaniel Bacon's Rebellion in Virginia" (1731), *The Maryland Muse* (1731), and "In Memory of Benedict Leonard Calvert" (1732), as well as another elegy (1732), written on the death of William Locke and signed "Ebenezer Cook, Poet Laureat." There is no subsequent record of him and he is thought to have died in 1732. (Cooke was, of course, the inspiration for John Barth's ribald and satirical novel, *The Sot-Weed Factor*, published in 1960.)[23]

That there was indeed a "second edition" of *The Sot-weed Factor*—or at least that one was intended—is indicated by a version of the poem printed in Cooke's *The Maryland Muse*[24] which is described as "The Third Edition." Moreover, there survive (written on the flyleaves of a copy of Sir Edward Coke's *Second Part of the Institutes of the Lawes of England*, 1642) four holograph drafts "design'd for a preface" to "this Second edition" of *The Sot-weed Factor*.

The signature "E. Cooke" appears between the second and third drafts.[25]

Cohen (following Lawrence Wroth) suggests an approximate time for the writing of the drafts. Because in them Cooke refers to "the unparallel'd friendship & hospitallity" accorded him "since his last arrival in yᵉ Land of Nod," it is logically assumed he was writing after his return to Maryland to establish permanent residence. The earliest certain date to which this can be ascribed is 1720. Further, because Cooke's intention to publish would have been dependent upon the availability of a press (first established in the colony by William Parks in 1726)[26], and on the basis of certain tobacco acts to which Cooke alludes, Cohen suggests the drafts for the preface to the intended "second edition" were written in 1727 or 1728.[27]

No such second edition has ever come to light, and Cohen validly observes that "the existence of four drafts 'design'd for a preface' to a second edition of *The Sot-weed Factor* does not prove that such an edition was ever published." However, he cautions that "scholars should not avoid the temptation to speculate on the possibility that a second edition once did exist."[28]

The latter suggestion (that all copies of the edition are lost) would seem preferable to the former (that it was never published) in at least one regard: an *unpublished* edition is really a contradiction in terms. Indeed, according to a source approximately contemporaneous with Cooke, Samuel Johnson's dictionary of 1755, *edition* means "Publication; generally with some revisal or correcting."

That Cooke intended not only publication but revision as well is clear from the drafts of his preface, in each of which he states that "the curse" (hurled against the colonists at the end of the original poem) is to be omitted from this second edition. Yet if the intended publication never materialized, then why is the 1731 version labeled "The Third Edition"? Surely both author and printer (thought to be Parks)[29] knew the meaning of the word *edition*, and it is doubtful either would have applied it—incorrectly and to the bewilderment of readers—to an unpublished revision.

Most important is the fact that a further, modified draft of the preface was actually published with Cooke's *Sotweed Redivivus*, printed by William Parks in 1730.[30] as Cohen says of this preface in comparison with the earlier drafts, "the duplicate words and similarities of phrases, of analogous structure, and of the repeated 'apology' are too great to be coincidental."[31] Indeed they are. For example, whereas the preface contains the phrase, "one Blast from the Critick's Mouth," a draft reads, "one blast from a Criticks mouth," and just as the preface ends, "as often as his Inclination or Interest shall prompt him," a draft concludes, "so oft as either his interest or [inc]lination prompts him."

Could *Sotweed Redivivus*, then, actually *be* the presumed "lost" second edition? At first sight, this possibility (which apparently never occurred to Cohen or others) might seem farfetched. Certainly *Sotweed Redivivus* differs from the original, the *Sot-weed Factor*, not only in title but significantly in content as well. It has, indeed, been considered "a sequel." Yet there is nothing that is necessarily dependent upon the reader's having read the earlier poem.

Rather, there are analogous passages so similar in form and wording as to seemingly belie the "sequel" notion. For example, in the 1708 version the sotweed factor sets off with his guide for a place

> In *Mary-Land* of high renown,
> Known by the Name of *Battle-Town*.
> . . . .
> Scarce had we enterd on the way,
> Which thro' thick Woods and Marshes lay.

Strikingly similar are these lines from *Sotweed Redivivus:*

> *To* Battle-Town, *the Author took his Way,*
> *That thro' thick Woods and Fenny Marshes lay . . .*

In fact, a number of lines and word groupings from the 1708 poem are repeated in *Sotweed Redivivus,* as James T. Pole has demonstrated (see Table 3).[32] The repetition of verbatim portions (no matter how much the poem is otherwise different) would seem exceedingly unusual for a sequel per se but entirely compatible with a replacement version.

While the adjective *redivivus* certainly permits the interpretation that the poem is a sequel, its precise meaning (according to the *Oxford English Dictionary*) is "Liable to revive; reappearing." It is thus similar in meaning to "second edition" in the sense of "*Sotweed* reappearing" or even "*Sotweed* reissued." In fact, some other works having *redivivus* in their titles—e.g., the *Smectymnuus Redivivus*—are not sequels but are simply later editions of the works.[33]

Table 3. Similar Word Groupings in *The Sot-weed Factor* and *Sotweed Redivivus*.

The Sot-weed Factor	*Sotweed Redivivus*
Planted at first, when Vagrant *Cain* His Brother had unjustly slain.	But *Copper-Coin*, like vagrant *Cain*, Wou'd never wander into *Spain*.
This said, the Rundlet up he threw, And bending backwards strongly drew.	This said, the Glass he upwards threw, And bending backwards, strongly drew.
Where I was instantly convey'd By one who pass'd for Chamber-Maid.	Where instantly I was convey'd, By one that pass'd for Chamber-Maid.
Curious to know from whence she came,	Curious to know from whence he came,
I prest her to declare her Name.	I boldly crav'd his Worship's Name.
I thence inferr'd *Phoenicians* old, Discover'd first with Vessels bold.	As the *Phoenicians* did of old, To plow the Seas in Vessels bold.
Could better bare the potent Juice.	Inspir'd by the potent Juice.
Rise *Oronooka*, rise, said I.	Rise, *Oroonoko*, rise, said I.
Till Midnight in her sable Vest, Persuaded Gods and Men to rest; And with a pleasing kind surprize, Indulg'd soft Slumbers to my Eyes.	'Till Midnight, in her Sable Vest, Persuaded *Gods* and *Men* to Rest; And with a pleasing kind Surprize, Indulg'd soft Slumber to my Eyes.
Fierce *Aethon* courser of the Sun Had half his Race exactly run.	As *Aethon*, Courser of the Sun, Had half his Race exactly run.
Agreeing for ten thousand weight, Of *Sot-weed* good and fit for freight.	Should be allow'd *Six Hundred* Weight, Of *sotweed* good, and fit for Freight.

If *Sotweed Redivivus* is *not* the "missing" second edition, and if the edition did not go unpublished, then we are left with a number of questions which seem all but unanswerable. For intance, we know that the drafted preface was intended for the second edition and that it was subsequently used (in a further draft form) for *Sotweed Redivivus*. If it was obviously not used for the presumed "missing" edition, we must question why that was so. In other words, we must suppose the following complex and puzzling scenario: that sometime in about 1728, Cooke wrote several drafts for a preface to a second edition; that he chose, for whatever unknown reason, to publish that edition *without* a preface or else with an entirely *new* one; that he then wrote and published a lengthy "sequel" to the original poem, borrowing many word groupings from it (an unusual act for anything other than a revision); that he affixed to the "sequel" a preface not originally intended for it but rather one planned *for another work;* that he then prepared a third edition of the original poem which could scarcely have been greatly different from the recently published second edition; and, finally, that no copies of the earlier (second) edition have survived.[34]

In contrast is the simpler hypothesis—and thus the preferred one according to "Occam's razor" (see Chapter 1)—that Cooke simply affixed the preface to the edition for which it was intended. This possibility seems further supported by a comparison of the drafts of the intended preface with the text of *Sotweed Redivivus.* In the drafts, as Cohen points out, Cooke draws an "analogy between a 'latter crop' of tobacco and his intended second edition" which "is developed, in part, through references to acts passed by the Maryland Assembly for improving the local staple."

Just such a concern with tobacco laws—notably absent from the first and third editions of *Sot-weed Factor*—permeates *Sotweed Redivivus.* This mutual concern, together with the common references to regulatory acts, is entirely consistent with the possibility that the preface for the "second edition" was indeed intended for *Sotweed Redivivus.* Certainly this possibly is strengthened measurably by the fact that a further draft of the preface *was* actually used for *Sotweed Redivivus.*

What may be said, then, against the new hypothesis? The strongest argument would appear to be that *Sotweed Redivivus* is too different in content to be regarded as another edition of *The Sot-weed Factor.* But this argument is weakened by the demonstrably similar passages in both works—similarities that would seem more in keeping with *Sotweed Redivivus*'s being a replacement version of the original poem that with its being a "sequel" per se.

To attempt to answer the question of why Cooke would wish to replace the original satire with *Sotweed Redivivus,* we must return again to the holograph drafts of the preface. From the first of these we learn that "some idle tattlers" had made ill-founded speculations concerning *The Sot-weed Factor.* Apparently Cooke's intention to republish the poem in the colonies (probably announced in order to obtain subscribers) had prompted some to suggest he was not the original author of "such Bombast" against the colonists. He avows that he indeed wrote the satire but disclaims, "ye Curse wch the Gent. yt Corrected ye press, was pleas'd to add, & in this Second edition is entirely omitted, in Consideration of yᵉ unparallell'd friendship & in who[se] hospitallity our Sottweed has met wᵗʰ since his last Voyage."

Just as Cooke seems to have catered shrewdly to his original (1708) English audience, he appears to have determined to do likewise with his American one—that is, to remove the offending curse (which he lamely attempts to attribute to the publisher). On reflection, he may have sensed that other portions might also be thought objectionable, as Cohen points out.[35] Whether or not the offending passages represented Cooke's personal feelings at the time they were written, they are such an integral part of *The Sotweed Factor* that only by creating a completely new version could they be eliminated.

Yet simply writing a new poem would not necessarily revoke the former one. What was needed was for "the sotweed poem" to be transformed (thus becoming a sort of recantation) into a new, distinctly American, edition, a *Sotweed Redivivus*. If it retained some vestiges of the first, so much the better.

But then why would Cooke so soon thereafter issue a "Third Edition," and why one so similar to the original? We can begin an answer by noting that if there were no missing second edition—or rather, if *Sotweed Redivivus* actually *were* the second edition—this would mean that *The Sot-weed Factor* had not been published since 1708 and then only in England. Publication of the *Sotweed Redivivus* might well have sparked the curiosity of many who had not actually seen the original, and Cooke—ever willing to produce (as he stated in the preface drafts) "merchantable ware"—could have seized the opportunity to capitalize on the demand.

In summary, the new hypothesis appears capable of consolidating various individual puzzles into a cohesive and coherent solution to the "perplexing" problem of the "second edition" of the *Sot-weed Factor*. If it is correct, then the "lost" edition has actually been in plain view for some two and a half centuries.

Recommended Works

Altick, Richard D. *The Scholar Adventurers*. New York: Macmillan, 1951. Chapters especially relevant to lost texts include "The Secret of the Ebony Cabinet," "Hunting for Manuscripts," and "Secrets in Cipher."

Beardsley, Niel F. "The Photography of Altered and Faded Manuscripts."

Library Journal 61 (1936): 96-99. Description of photographic techniques for enhancing old writing.

Ceram, C.W., ed. *Hands on the Past: Pioneer Archaeologists Tell Their Own Story.* New York: Knopf, 1966. Includes case studies of deciphering ancient texts, treats advances in computer decipherment, etc.

Gardner, Martin. *Codes, Ciphers, and Secret Writing.* New York: Pocket Books, 1972. Good introduction to different kinds of secret writing.

Kirkham, E. Kay. *The Handwriting of American Records for a Period of 300 Years.* Logan, Utah: Everton, 1973. Guide to reading old handwriting.

Thoyt, E.E. *How to Decipher and Study Old Documents*, 2d ed., 1903. Detroit: Gale Research, 1974. Basic guide to decipherment of old manuscripts.

Hawthorne's "Veiled Lady"

A history can only be as accurate as its sources, for if they are incomplete, biased, or spurious, then any view predicated on them can scarcely be otherwise. Therefore, source study is a frequent activity of the historical sleuth.

Consider, for example, *The Horn Papers* of western Pennsylvania historiography.[1] Largely "transcriptions" of alleged diaries of Jacob and Christopher Horn that were since "lost," they were a veritable mine of information. They yielded valuable data on ordinary settlers as well as on leaders—like Christopher Gist and Jonathan Hager—of the western movement, filling in many important gaps in those persons' lives. Unfortunately, investigation soon revealed that the diaries and accompanying papers contained anachronistic wording (e.g., "hometown"), as well as internal discrepancies, historically incorrect statements, and other problems, including biographical anomalies. According to investigators:

An authentic diary would be true throughout, not just in a majority of its entries. It would be true, in all instances where the writer was in a position to know the truth. A genuine diary might, indeed, contain a false statement because the writer was misinformed, because he recorded hearsay that was in error, or because his judgment was faulty. But an authentic diary would under no circumstances record the appearance and activities in the writer's company of a person when that person is known to have been elsewhere or after he is known to have died. A single instance of this kind would cast doubt on the authenticity of a diary even though every other entry were correct, for it would unquestionably demonstrate that the document had been tampered with. *The Horn Papers* contain not one but many such biographical irregularities, and they form, perhaps, the most important single body of *prima facie* evidence against the manuscripts.[2]

In short, the mine of information was largely fool's gold, the few genuine nuggets merely borrowings from published sources, including Boyd Crumrine's *Old Virginia Court House at Augusta Town, Near Washington, Pennsylvania, 1776-1777*. Maps among *The Horn Papers* were shown to have details derived from modern cartography, particularly U.S. Geological Survey maps from which portions may even have been traced. The purveyor of the fake documents, one W.F. Horn, attempted to counter skepticism by citing corroborative sources, but many of those turned out to be nonexistent publications.

As a result of the "noxious influences" of the spurious papers, many genealogists were deceived, and the National Society of the Daughters of the American Revolution eventually had to take measures to deal with them. The historians who debunked the papers concluded that "the poison works on" and that "undoubtedly, for years to come some unwary individuals will continue to be misled by the documents' fascinating historical fictions."[3]

In a somewhat similar fashion, the tale about George Washington hacking down the cherry tree was planted in *The Life of George Washington* by its author, Mason Locke ("Parson") Weems (1759-1825). From there it spread its branches into many published works. Weems claimed the story had been communicated to him by an "excellent" if elderly lady, and he characterized it as "too valuable to be lost, and too true to be doubted."[4] Actually, Parson Weems's source was not the product of venerable oral tradition as it had seemed. According to Curtis D. MacDougall, "Origin of the cherry-tree myth has been traced to a story by Dr. James Beattie, *The Minstrel*, published in London in 1799, which Weems plagiarized. The same book also contained the anecdote of cabbage seeds which grew up to form a person's name, another credited by Weems to Washington."[5]

Just as discovering the true source of the cherry tree tale effectively debunks it, establishing a credible source for some historical allegation can have the opposite effect. For example, I was once skeptical of a folktale that was laying claim to historical fact. It had a condemned man seated atop his coffin as a wagon carried him to the gallows—a detail that seemed suspiciously dramatic. But doubt turned to acceptance when a newspaper was found stating that, a month earlier in another city, two condemned men were conveyed "seated upon their coffins and guarded by the Sheriff's posse of one hundred well armed men."[6] Further, a treatise on hanging indicates this was a long-standing custom.[7]

Literary scholars also study sources—not to judge writers' veracity but to measure their originality, shed light on other aspects of their creative processes, obtain help in clarifying particular passages, and for other benefits, including the establishment of literary relationships which can serve as preparation for writing a literary history. (Such a history—Sir Herbert Grierson and J.C. Smith's *Critical History of English Poetry* is an example—treats derivations and relationships between particular authors and literary schools, which are chronologically presented in order to provide historical perspectives.)[8]

The sources may be literary or nonliterary. Of the former, Shakespearean examples include the story of *As You Like It*, which came from a Thomas Lodge novel, and *The Comedy of Errors* for which a Roman comedy served as the source.[9]

Of the other, nonliterary type there is, for instance, Edgar Allan Poe's "The Mystery of Marie Roget," which was a tale derived from American newspaper accounts of the death of Mary Rogers.[10] Joseph Conrad also used as sources for his fiction many actual incidents, as well as characters drawn from real life,[11] and Charles Dickens was another who frequently drew upon nonliterary sources.

Indeed, much scholarly ink has been expended in futile attempts to identify literary sources for Dickens's "spontaneous combustion" episode in *Bleak House* (1853), wherein the sinister Mr. Krook perishes by a fiery fate. Among the candidates have been Charles Brockden Brown's *Wieland* (1798), Frederick Marryat's *Jacob Faithful* (1834), and Herman Melville's *Redburn* (1849).[12]

However, Wiley conceded that "if Dickens owes the suggestion to other novelists, he owes little else."[13] In fact, Dickens—in chapter 33 of *Bleak House*, again in the Preface, and yet again in a letter to George Henry Lewes—actually listed his sources.[14] Of greatest significance is the gruesome account of the immolation of the Countess Bandi, which had appeared in the *Gentleman's Magazine* and other publications. Dickens specifically states, in the Preface, "The appearances beyond all rational doubt observed in that case, are the appearances observed in Mr. Krook's case." Indeed Dickens relied on the account of the case for specific details. For example, he wrote that on the windowsill was a "thick yellow liquor . . . which is offensive to the touch and sight and more offensive to the smell. A stagnant, sickening oil." Similarly, the source account states that "from the lower part of the window, trickled down a greasy, loathsome, yellowish liquor with an unusual stink."[15]

Even if we did not have Dickens's sources from his own statements, we could at least identify this one from its close correspondence with the unusual imagery and distinctive phrasing ("yellow liquor") in *Bleak House*. As Richard D. Altick writes in *The Art of Literary Research:*

A small, isolated similarity of phrase proves little if anything. But the likelihood of direct relationship grows if two passages virtually match, or contain peculiarities (unusual words or idioms, out-of-the-way images or images with unaccustomed details or uses) which are associated only with the two specific authors under consideration. Similarly with the various non-verbal resemblances. Mere occasional likenesses of plot, character, artistic form, or ideas are individually of small significance, unless they all point unmistakably in the same direction. The likelihood of direct borrowing increases with the quantity of evidence.[16]

The accompanying table amplifies the evidence from Dickens's sources. Unlike Krook, the countess was *not* given to intoxication. But that element is common to other cases read by Dickens, and his immediate source (as shown in Table 4) was probably the Millet case of 1725 which Dickens also specifically mentioned in his letter to Lewes.

I believe Dickens drew from one other case. His description of Krook's remains as resembling a "log of wood" covered "with white ashes" repeats those exact words from a case Dickens specifically referred to in his letter to Lewes, an 1835 account of the death of Mrs. Grace Pett (again see table).[17]

The lesson from Dickens on matching artistic work with source can be useful when we turn to an American writer who, like his British contemporary, also frequently employed nonliterary sources. In many instances the sources for people and incidents in Nathaniel Hawthorne's fiction have been identified, but the model—if indeed there ever was one—for an important character in one major novel has previously been unknown.

In the autumn of 1851, Nathaniel Hawthorn settled with his wife, Sophia, and his young son and infant daughter at West Newton in

Table 4. A Comparison of Dickens's Spontaneous Combustion Episode with Accounts of Cases He Read.

Dickens, Bleak House	Accounts Known to Dickens
". . . the fact of Mr. Krooks being 'continual in liquor.' " (392) [Tony:] "He'll have drunk himself blind . . . He's been at it all day." (397)	The victim reportedly "got intoxicated every day." (Millet case)
"[T]here is a smouldering suffocating vapour in the room. . . ." (402)	"The foetid odour and smoke . . . almost suffocated some of the neighbors. . . ." (Pett case)
[Mr. Guppy:]"See how the soot's falling. See here on my arm! See again, on the table here! Con-found the stuff, it won't blow off—smears, like black fat." (p. 398) "Fah! Here's more of this hateful soot hanging about." (400)	"The air in the room had soot floating in it . . . the whole furniture spread over with moist ash-coloured soot. . . . In the room above, the said soot flew about. . . ." "[The ashes] left in the hand a greasy and stinking moisture. . . ." (Bandi case)
On the window-sill, a "thick yellow liquor . . . which is offensive to the touch and sight and more offensive to the smell. A stagnant, sickening oil. . . . (401) . . . it slowly drips, and creeps alway down the bricks; here, lies in a little thick nauseous pool." (402)	". . . [F]rom the lower part of the window, trickled down a greasy, loathsome, yellowish liquor with an unusual stink." (Bandi case)
". . . and a dark greasy coating on the walls and ceiling." (402)	"This soot even got into a neighboring kitchen, hung on its walls and utensils. . . ." (Bandi case)
The remains resembled "the cinder of a small charred and broken log of wood sprinkled with white ashes, or is it coal? (403)	The body "had the appearance of a log of wood consumed by a fire. . . . The trunk . . . resembled a heap of coals covered with white ashes." (Pett case)

eastern Massachusetts. During the subsequent winter he wrote a novel, published in 1852, that was his third in as many years. Titled *The Blithedale Romance*, it was a study of a utopian community that grew out of his own residency at Brook Farm in 1841.

That idealistic community of writers and reformers (or "philanthropists" as they were called) had been organized in that year by the Rev. George Ripley, a former Unitarian minister and an editor of the critical literary monthly, *The Dial*. During the six months the then-bachelor Hawthorne spent at Brook Farm, he milked cows, chopped wood, turned a grindstone, loaded carts with manure, and penned letters and entries in his notebook that reflected on the life there. However, by June 1 he was impelled to write, "this present life of mine gives me an antipathy to pen and ink." And by September 1 he was back at his mother's in Salem.[18] A decade later, while at work on the *Blithedale* manuscript, Hawthorne was using his notebooks—particularly his Brook Farm entries—as a source-book for characters and incidents. For example, a description of a "picnic party in the woods" (of September 28, 1841)—replete with costumed figures of an Indian chief, gypsy fortune-teller, goddess Diana, and others—was reworked into the unmistakably similar encounter of chapter 24, "The Masqueraders." According to Arlin Turner,

Other episodes of the romance which were lifted from the author's Brook Farm observations—directly from his notebooks in some instances—are Coverdale's arrival in a snowstorm and his illness, his farewell to the pigs, Priscilla's riding the ox and her upsetting the load of hay. Among the smaller matters brought over from Brook Farm are the various kinds of work on the farm, the neighbors' laughing at the farmers as they learned to milk, the walks in the woods, the gathering of wild flowers, the horn blown at rising time each morning, and the attendance at the theater during a visit to the city. In like manner such elements of setting as the houses at the farm, Eliot's pulpit, and Coverdale's hermitage in the grapevine belong to both Brook Farm and Blithedale.[19]

Hawthorne also drew on a number of notebook entries both before Brook farm (including an 1838 description of a view from a Boston hotel window) and afterward (including a May 7, 1850, account of a saloon visit that supplied details for chapter 21). Continues Turner,

Still more literally than in any of these instances, the episode of recovering Zenobia's body originated in the author's observations. On July 9, 1845, when Hawthorne lived at the Old Manse, he was roused in the night to help search for the body of Martha Hunt, who had drowned herself in the Concord River. His notebook supplied what he needed later for his fictional account, even such symbolic details as the position in which Zenobia's body had grown rigid and the wound inflicted by the pole which Hollingsworth used in bringing her body to the surface of the water.[20]

Other characterizations in *Blithedale* had originals, of varying degrees of closeness, despite Hawthorne's prefatory insistence that the characters were "entirely fictitious" and that they "might have been looked for at Brook Farm, but, by some accident, never made their appearance there." Certainly, Priscilla was closely modeled on Brook Farm's "little seamstress from Boston," described in an entry of October 9, 1841. Silas Foster and Hollingsworth are each thought to have been drawn, in part, from multiple models, and Hawthorne himself yielded much that became Coverdale.[21]

Given such an extensive use of real-life models for people and events in *Blithedale*, one must wonder whether the "Veiled Lady" of the romance—a trance medium exploited by a charlatan—might likewise have had an original. Might she not, in fact, have been based on an actual stage performer who toured New England in Hawthorne's time—a stage performer who, like the Veiled Lady, was of the trickster variety?

In beginning our search, we should note that, apart from his obvious familiarity with the trappings of occult magic and sorcerers,[22] Hawthorne had a keen eye for another kind of magic—that of the "juggler, with his tricks of mimic witchcraft" (as he wrote in *The Scarlet Letter*). In *Blithedale*, in describing "one of those lyceumhalls of which almost every village has now its own," he says, "besides the winter course of lectures, there is a rich and varied series of other exhibitions. Hither comes the ventriloquist, with all his mysterious tongues; the thaumaturgist, too, with his miraculous transformations of plates, doves, and rings, his pancakes smoking in your hat, and his cellar of choice liquors represented in one small bottle."[23]

This description demonstrates that Hawthorne was actually drawing quite precisely from real life. Ventriloquists did often perform in the lyceum-halls and frequently shared the bill with prestidigitators. As to the general classes of magic which Hawthorne represented as "transformations of plates, doves, and rings," these were the conjurers' stock-in-trade and scarcely require any elaboration, except perhaps to cite the wonderworkings of Signor Antonio Blitz, described on the handbill for his 1835 performance in Cambridge, Massachusetts, as "The Saxon Dishes and Goblets of the Great" plus the "Dance of Six Dinner Plates." Daniel Webster, Millard Fillmore, and Martin Van Buren were among Blitz's admirers.[24]

However, with those "pancakes smoking in your hat," Hawthorne is no longer dealing in generalities. Delisle, the flamboyant French conjurer, was cooking omelets in borrowed hats as early as 1751. And Monsieur Gyngell, the early nineteenth-century British fairgrounds magician, requested "the loan of a hat, merely to boil a pudding in!" The 1876 text, *Modern Magic* by "Professor Hoffman" details the secret of "The Cake (or Pudding) in the Hat." Indeed, if we are to believe the 1822 handbill of "Ingleby, Emperor of all the Conjurers, from the Lyceum London" (who was then performing "at the Raven Assembly Room, Bridgnorth"), his magical production was of "Well-Made Pancakes" conjured up out of "a pint of Water, one pint of Flour, and two new-laid Eggs, without any deception whatever"!—all this poured into "any Gentleman's Hat" and cooked in one minute over a candle.[25]

Like the "smoking pancakes" feat, the "cellar of choice liquors represented in one small bottle" was a popular conjuring item in Hawthorne's own time. The trick is illustrated on a poster for "Professor Anderson's Grand Soirees Mysterieuse." Known as "The Wizard of the North," this great Scotch magician first toured America in 1851, the year in which *The Blithedale Romance* was begun.[26] Earlier, the masterful Ludwig Leopold Dobler (1801-1864)—who performed in Russia, Holland, Germany, France and England, as well as his native Austria, before retiring in 1848— featured the bottle trick, as perhaps did others. In his version, Dobler "first filled the bottle with water, then poured out champagne, sherry, hock and other wines to serve to thirsty spectators. To prove the bottle was an ordinary, unprepared object he smashed it after the show of magic wine, and, for an added surprise, pulled from it a spectator's handkerchief, which he had borrowed earlier in the evening."[27]

I have dwelt at some length upon Hawthorne's brief mention of "the thaumaturgist" in order to demonstrate what might not otherwise have been apparent, that in a particular instance Hawthorne was accurately portraying a typical traveling conjurer, and also to set the stage, as it were, for considering that Hawthorne's characterization of the Veiled Lady was similarly drawn from a real-life model or models.

In *Blithedale*, characters are frequently described in phantasmagoric terms, for example as "vaporous and spectre-like," or as an "apparition." Again, "They called her [Priscilla] ghost-child, and said that she could indeed vanish when she pleased. . . . in the first gray of twilight, she lost all the distinctness of her outline; and if you followed the dim thing into a dark corner, behold! she was not there."[28]

Two clues combine to suggest a source of Hawthorne's inspiration for such presentations of visible, if ethereal, fantasies. The first clue is found in *Blithedale*, where we again find Priscilla, this time in the village-hall in the guise of the Veiled Lady. After she comes "gliding upon the platform," she takes her seat and, "sitting there, in such visible obscurity, it was perhaps as much like the actual presence of a disembodied spirit as anything that *stage trickery* could devise (my italics)."[29] The second clue comes from *The Scarlet Letter:* "Reminiscences . . . came swarming back upon her . . . ; one picture precisely as vivid as another. . . . Possibly, it was an instinctive device of her spirit, to relieve itself, by the *exhibition of these phantasmagoric forms*, from the cruel weight and hardness of the reality (emphasis added)."[30]

Now Hawthorne's use of the word *phantasmagoric* is greatly instructive. According to the *Oxford English Dictionary*, the term *phantasmagoria* was "invented for the exhibition of optical illusions produced chiefly by means of the magic lantern, first exhibited in London in 1802. . . . In [the stage magician] Philipstal's [or de Philipsthal's] 'phantasmagoria,' the figures were made rapidly to increase and decrease in size, to advance and retreat, dissolve, vanish, and pass into each other, in a manner then considered marvellous." The term soon came to apply to "a shifting series or succession of phantoms or imaginary figures, as seen in a dream or fevered condition, as called up by the imagination, or as created by literary description." However, used metaphorically or not, the term does refer to de Philipsthal's original ghost show—a fact Hawthorne must surely have known. Indeed, in *The House of the Seven Gables* (1851) he speaks of "a ghostly or phantasmagoric reflection,"[31] and in connection with the Veiled Lady (above) he specifically mentioned "stage trickery."

If the characterization of Priscilla (the Veiled Lady) as a "disembodied spirit" was partly owing to de Philipsthal's "phantasmagoria" (indeed, de Philipsthal's advertisement referred to "Disembodied Spirits") that is only a partial source. Consider how the Veiled Lady is styled: She was a "hitherto inexplicable phenomenon"[32] whom "the bills had announced . . . at the corners of every street."[33] She

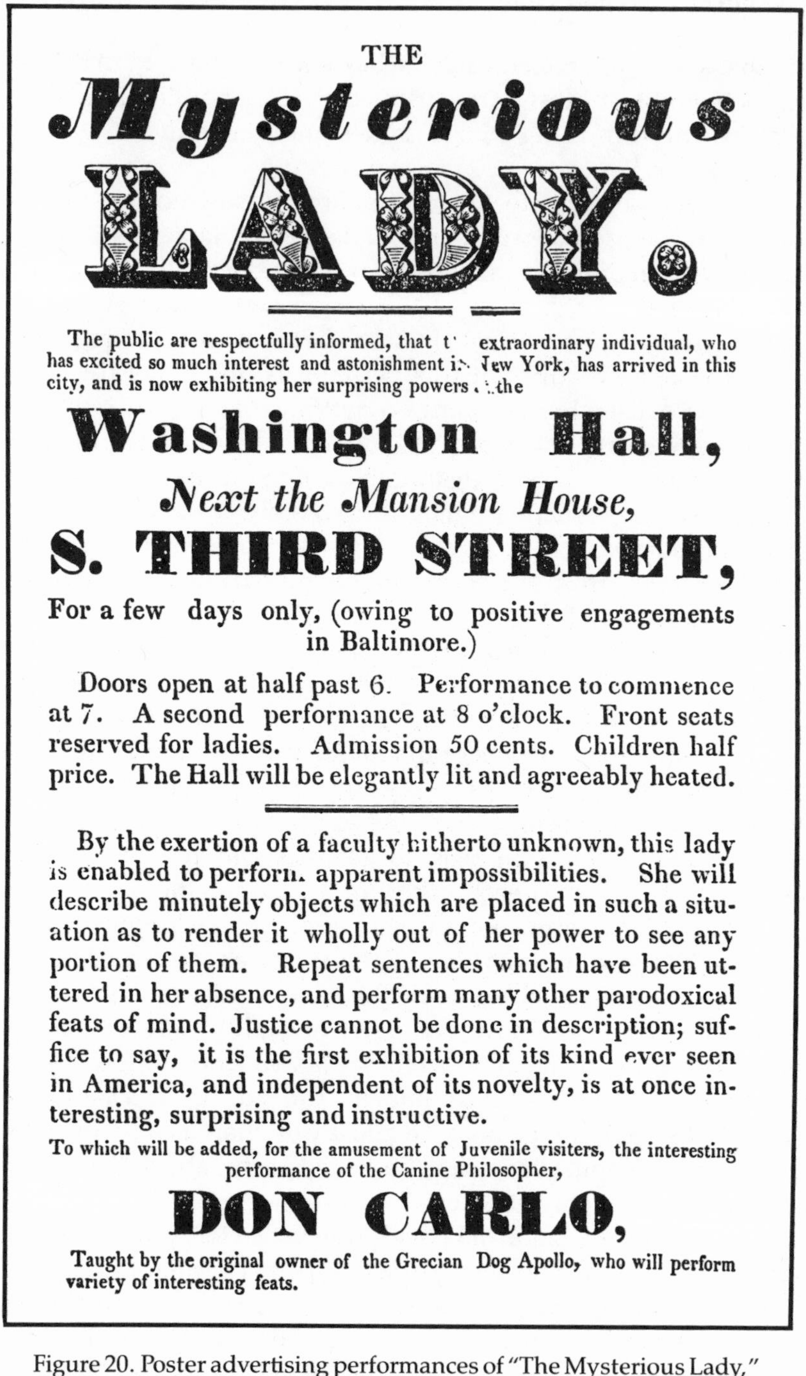

THE
Mysterious
LADY.

The public are respectfully informed, that t' extraordinary individual, who has excited so much interest and astonishment i: Jew York, has arrived in this city, and is now exhibiting her surprising powers ٫ ٫the

Washington Hall,
Next the Mansion House,
S. THIRD STREET,

For a few days only, (owing to positive engagements in Baltimore.)

Doors open at half past 6. Performance to commence at 7. A second performance at 8 o'clock. Front seats reserved for ladies. Admission 50 cents. Children half price. The Hall will be elegantly lit and agreeably heated.

By the exertion of a faculty hitherto unknown, this lady is enabled to perform apparent impossibilities. She will describe minutely objects which are placed in such a situation as to render it wholly out of her power to see any portion of them. Repeat sentences which have been uttered in her absence, and perform many other parodoxical feats of mind. Justice cannot be done in description; suffice to say, it is the first exhibition of its kind ever seen in America, and independent of its novelty, is at once interesting, surprising and instructive.

To which will be added, for the amusement of Juvenile visiters, the interesting performance of the Canine Philosopher,

DON CARLO,

Taught by the original owner of the Grecian Dog Apollo, who will perform variety of interesting feats.

Figure 20. Poster advertising performances of "The Mysterious Lady," who probably served as the model for Hawthorne's "Veiled Lady" character.

is presented in a "hall of exhibition"[34]—where also perform the ventriloquist and thaumaturgist—by a "magician" wearing "oriental robes."[35] even from a great distance she can hear "the lowest whispered breath"[36] through her "gift of second sight and prophecy,"[37] which in fact is nothing more than the result of "juggling tricks."[38] And we are told that "the interest of the spectator was further wrought up by the enigma of her identity"[39]—all this taking place before "the epoch of the rapping spirits."[40]

For comparison, consider this performance in Philadelphia (as well as New York, Baltimore, and presumably elsewhere, possibly even Boston) in the 1840s. Appearing at the Washington Hall and advertised by playbills was a female performer identified *only* as "The Mysterious Lady," an "extraordinary individual." The advertisement (see Figure 20) continued:

By the exertion of a faculty hitherto unknown, this lady is enabled to perform apparent impossibilities. She will describe minutely objects which are placed in such a situation as to render it wholly out of her power to see any portion of them. Repeat sentences which have been uttered in her absence, and perform many other paradoxical feats of mind. Justice cannot be done in description; suffice to say, it is the first exhibition of its kind ever seen in America, and independent of its novelty, is at once interesting, surprising and instructive.[41]

The feats attributed to the Mysterious Lady represent what in stage magicians' parlance is termed a "second-sight routine." This very old trick involves a partner, the magician, who works the routine with the medium, secretly conveying to her by clever means the information on chosen objects and whispered utterances.[42]

Could the Mysterious Lady have served as a model for Hawthorne's Veiled Lady? Certainly the parallels are striking. First of all, only a very, very few early American performers were females. I know of no female stage magicians until much later in the century, with the single exception of the Mysterious Lady—who was almost certainly not a *magicienne* proper but a subject exhibited by a magician.

Second, whereas virtually all magical performers were billed by their own names—or at least stage names—the term "The Mysterious Lady" is from a different mold. Her billing is strikingly similar to that of "The Veiled Lady" since only the adjectives "mysterious" versus "veiled" are different and these are, of course, synonyms.

Also, both concealed their identities: Hawthorne's character used a veil; the mysterious lady "presented her back to the spectators but never revealed her face."[43]

Further, in addition to being similarly designated, both were advertised by playbills and presented in exhibition halls (rather than in drawing rooms like so many spiritualists). Moreover, their magical powers were described in almost identical terms—the Veiled Lady as a "hitherto inexplicable phenomenon" and the Mysterious Lady as performing "by the exertion of a faculty hitherto unknown."

Hawthorne tells us that the Veiled Lady accomplished her magical effects by "juggling tricks." And Milbourne Christopher obviously thinks the same of the Mysterious Lady's effects since he includes her in his book on performers of magic tricks.

Of real significance is the fact that both ladies performed similar routines, and these were clearly second-sight routines: Hawthorne specifically speaks of the Veiled Lady's "gift [actually trick] of second sight"; and the Mysterious Lady obviously performed the magician's usual second-sight routine since she could "describe minutely objects which are placed in such a way as to render it wholly out of her power to see any portion of them."

The respective routines specifically included feats of a virtually identical nature: The Veiled Lady could—even from a great distance—hear "the lowest whispered breath"; and similarly, the Mysterious Lady was able to "repeat sentences which had been uttered in her absence." This particular trick—which goes beyond the mere identification of an object—represents a rather striking similarity between the two routines.

Such parallels gain added weight when taken together. (We recall Altick's statement: "The likelihood of direct borrowing increases with the quantity of evidence.") They might mean less if it could be shown that such performers as the Mysterious Lady were common, but I have been able to discover only the single one in Hawthorne's time, and that lends some credibility to her claim that her act was "the first exhibition of its kind ever seen in America."

Also we have to consider the time frame. The Veiled Lady's performances took place, Hawthorne writes, before "the epoch of the rapping spirits"—that is, before the Fox Sisters produced "the rap heard round the world" in 1848; and the Mysterious Lady's performances in New England were, Christopher says, "in the 1840's." [44]

We must acknowledge that Priscilla was not drawn from a single model but like certain other *Blithedale* characters was a composite. Recall that as Priscilla she had an original in the young seamstress at Brook Farm. As the Veiled Lady, she seems to have had another original in the Mysterious Lady—just as Silas Foster and Hollingsworth were drawn from more than a single model.

While the Mysterious Lady made no appearance in Hawthorne's journals, his letter of October 18, 1841, was a reply to his wife-to-be about certain instances of mediumistic phenomena she had reported to him.

> Belovedest, my spirit is moved to talk to thee to-day about these magnetic miracles and to beseech thee to take no part in them. I am unwilling that a power should be exercised on thee of which we know neither the origin nor the consequence, and the phenomena of which seem rather calculated to bewilder us, than to teach us any truths about the present or future state of being. . . . Without distrusting that the phenomena which thou tellest me of and others as remarkable, have really occurred, I think that they are to be accounted for as the result of a physical and material, not of a spiritual, influence. [45]

The couple's exchange of letters demonstrates their interest in such phenomena at that time, his from a thoughtful and apparently informed opinion.

If it is correct to identify the Mysterious Lady as the original for the analogous figure in *Blithedale*, then we are beneficiaries of the new data in several respects. First of all we have a significant further instance of Hawthorne's use of a source—and in so recognizing, we become even more acutely aware that the artistic whole is far more than the mere sum of selected parts. As Arlin Turner explains,

> It was not Hawthorne's habit to write stories or novels about people or places or events, or about social institutions or social philosophies, though these of course were the matter of his fiction and often furnished the starting point in the development of a story in his mind. He wrote about ideas, usually about ideas with a moral tincture and with a bearing on human conduct and human character. The inclusive idea of *The Blithedale Romance* is brotherhood; and what the author had observed at Brook Farm,

including his own activities and thoughts and feelings simply furnished
the paraphernalia for handling and displaying that idea.⁴⁶

Second, the putative model represents yet another instance of Hawthorne's employing a nonliterary source, one drawn from contemporary life (whether or not from his own experience). It therefore
underscores Turner's observation that, with *Blithedale*, Hawthorne
"moved out of the colonial past in which he had set most of his
earlier fiction."⁴⁷ An added reliance on contemporary sources
might be a consequence of Hawthorne's changed perspective.

In addition, the evidence of the Mysterious Lady combines with
other indicators such as the pancakes-in-the-hat trick to suggest
Hawthorne may actually have attended magical performances. At
least, he showed an interest in them and demonstrated both an
ability and a willingness to portray them with fidelity of detail. He
also took pains to differentiate between the legitimate conjurer's act
and one imbued with pseudoscience and hokum, transforming the
latter into a situation in which Priscilla is a medium exploited by a
diabolical Professor Westervelt.

Hawthorne's apparent interest in magical performances is a
logical outgrowth of his larger concern with illusion versus reality.
It is a persistent theme in his fiction, common to such stories as
"Feathertop; a Moralized Legend" (the tale of a scarecrow who is
symbolic of empty-headed types but who at least recognizes he is
an illusion), "The Hall of Fantasy" (a museum of unrealistic schemes,
perpetual motion machines, and castles in the air), and "The Artist
of the Beautiful" (the story of a man whose all-consuming goal is the
fashioning of an eerily realistic automaton butterfly).

In *Blithedale* the theme is ubiquitous.⁴⁸ Intriguingly, in the Preface Hawthorne calls attention to the theme in terms of his own
creative process, and so acknowledges his use of sources drawn
from real life. As he states, referring to Brook Farm: "The author
does not wish to deny that he had this community in his mind, and
that (having had the good fortune, for a time, to be personally
connected with it) he has occasionally availed himself of his actual
reminiscences, in the hope of giving a more life-like tint to the
fancy-sketch in the following pages. He begs it to be understood,
however, that he has considered the institution itself as not less
fairly the subject of fictitious handling than the imaginary personages whom he has introduced there." He adds that he has

attempted "merely to establish a theatre, a little removed from the highway of ordinary travel, where the creatures of his brain may play their phantasmagorical antics, without exposing them to too close a comparison with the actual events of real lives."[49] Hawthorne is obviously being somewhat coy as to just what is "fictitious" and what is "real." Nor should that be surprising for one who deliberately mined contemporary reality for his fiction.[50]

Recommended Works

Altick, Richard D. *The Art of Literary Research.* New York: Norton, 1975. Research guide for serious students of literature; includes information on source study.

MacDougall, Curtis D. *Hoaxes.* New York: Dover, 1958. Classic text on historical and other types of hoaxes, revealing true sources behind many spurious (i.e., plagiarized or forged) works.

Middleton, Arthur Pierce, and Douglas Adair. "The Mystery of the Horn Papers." *William and Mary Quarterly,* 3d ser., 4 (Oct. 1947): 409-43. Investigative report on spurious historical papers.

Stallman, R.W. "The Scholar's Net: Literary Sources." *College English* 17 (1955): 20-27. Scholarly discussion of literary influences and source identifications.

Pseudoscience and the Shroud

Investigated with John F. Fischer

Scientific analysis, not itself a genre of historical mysteries but rather a body of technology applicable to many different genres, is indispensable to the investigator. Quite often it can be a deciding factor in resolving some important historical question, as suggested in previous chapters.

Microchemical analyses, for example, can be useful in questioned-document cases. As well, they are used to determine what pigments and binding media were used in paintings, and for many other identifications.[1]

Emission spectroscopy is another technique used to analyze materials when a tiny amount can be spared. The sample is heated to the glowing point, and then the light is passed through the prism in a spectroscope so that its distinctive spectrum can be identified. In this manner, an "ancient bronze" was shown to have been made of almost pure zinc, a metal that was unavailable to the Romans who supposedly made it.[2]

Nondestructive tests are employed when, as in the case of a rare metal coin or a precious porcelain artifact, not even a tiny sample can be sacrificed. For example, electron-beam analysis, which can analyze microscopic areas, was used to test the tiny pieces of glass making up a three-fourths-inch Roman mosaic plaque.[3] And x-ray fluorescence spectroscopy, which indicates surface composition of an artifact, has been employed for such purposes as distinguishing between imported and native cobalt in the blue glazes of Chinese pottery.[4]

An example of the importance of ordinary x-ray photography was given in chapter 6, with the case of the ostensibly fifteenth-century triptych that was revealed to have been constructed with modern hardware. As well, the radiograph showed that under-neath the painting and gilding was wood that was worm-eaten *before* those materials were applied. X-rays of paintings can reveal creative changes, made by the artist in the course of his work, that would probably not have been done by a mere copyist. Occasionally x-rays reveal an entire painting lurking under the surface. Beneath a sixteenth-century *Adoration of the Maji,* for instance, was found a *Holy Family* by the same artist, Jacob Jordaens, and underneath an "El Greco" was an old painting upon which the modern forgery had been done.[5]

Infrared photography—used with dramatic success to read age-darkened portions of the Dead Sea Scrolls—has many additional applications. Museum curators employ it to detect restoration on tapestries, for example, and to reveal designs on pottery and other artifacts that may have become invisible to the eye.[6] *Aerial* infrared photography has also been employed by archaeologists to detect various land scars, associated with ancient village sites, that neither the unaided eye nor ordinary photo is able to detect.[7] Other non-destructive tests include ultraviolet radiation, (shown earlier in Figures 18 and 19 for enhancing faded writing), x-ray diffraction analysis (employed in identfying crystalline compounds),[8] laser light (which may reveal traces not detected by ultraviolet or in-frared),[9] and many others.

Scientific techniques to determine the age of an artifact include radiocarbon dating of organic materials (discussed in chapter 2), thermoluminescent testing (particularly important in dating pot-tery),[10] and various other methods. The presence of materials used in making an artifact (such as machine-made nails, celluloid, or certain pigments in paint) can also assist in age determination.

Some of the analytical techniques we have been discussing were applied to a group of heretofore "lost" paintings bearing the signature of the Dutch master, Jan Vermeer (1632-1675). The result was scientific proof that they were actually fakes, rendered by "the forger supreme," Han van Meegeren (briefly alluded to in chapters 6 and 7).

The story began with the 1945 arrest of Van Meegeren in Am-sterdam on a charge of "collaboration with the enemy." Within weeks, however, the jailed painter was claiming that the *Christ and the Adultress* he had sold to the Nazi leader Göring was his own work—not a national treasure; he had merely signed Vermeer's name to it. To silence skeptics, who believed a mediocre artist was lying to avoid serious punishment for treason, Van Meegeren produced yet another "Vermeer," *The Young Christ*, behind bars.[11]

Eventually it was learned that Van Meegeren had turned out not only fake Vermeers but also bogus works by the master's Dutch contemporaries: Pieter de Hooch, Frans Hals, and others. He had used old canvases, mixed paint from natural pigments (including the true ultramarine that was a Vermeer favorite), and developed effective artificial aging techniques. (He used a mixture of phenol and formaldehyde to harden his paint like that three centuries old. He was even able to simulate the craquelure associated with age.)

Rather than copy known works, however, Van Meegeren created new paintings. According to one commentator,

with great skill he had cunningly imitated the style of Vermeer and had painted works that the experts might be expected to think would turn up one day. Besides being a master of techniques, the wily Van Meegeren was also a student of art history. He knew that most of the Dutch painters of Vermeer's time had painted at least some New Testament scenes. But if Vermeer had followed the trend of his time, his biblical paintings had either been lost or destroyed—with the exception of one early work. Yet the art experts hoped more might be discovered. Indeed, Van Meegeren "discovered" them for the world of art, and, by providing what the experts were ready to accept, diverted suspicion. Was he to be tried for the signatures or the paintings? It was an interesting legal question, and, in fact, he was eventually tried for both.[12]

Belatedly, scientists reexamined the paintings. Whereas prior study had been comparatively superficial—consisting of identification of some pigments and tests of paints for their resistance to certain solvents—the paintings were now subjected to a panoply of analyses. Further microchemical, microscopic, radiographic, spectroscopic, and other tests were carried out. As a result, traces of formaldehyde and phenol were detected, and the presence of cobalt blue, a pigment not known until 1802, was discovered. Residues of black ink were even found in the cracks of the varnish where it had been placed to simulate the grime of centuries.

At length, Van Meegeren, who had revenged himself upon the very critics who dismissed his early paintings, received a relatively light sentence of one year's imprisonment. Although he died of a heart attack a month after sentencing, his legacy remains: It is a lesson for today's historical detectives on the value of thorough scientific examination.[13]

However, it is not just in detecting forgeries and dating artifacts that science can aid the investigator. Consider the creative thinking of officials at the Museum of History and Science in Louisville, Kentucky: They commissioned a forensic anthropologist, Dr. Virginia Smith (who assisted in the Demjanjuk case, chapter 4), to reconstruct the features of an ancient Egyptian mummy.

The remains, dating from ca. 1400 B.C., are those of a young woman of about twenty, known as Then-Hotep. X-rays, made in 1985, indicated the petite woman may have been stoned to death—for doing "something wicked," opined a museum spokesperson.

For the restoration her skull (which became detached from its body during a 1937 flood) was first duplicated by casting. Then Smith inserted glass eyes into the sockets of the plaster skull, and at strategic points over its surface she attached small tissue-depth markers. These were connected with strips of clay, and finally the detailed features were modeled. Meanwhile, museum experts researched ancient Egyptian hairstyles in order to decide how to complete the reconstruction.[14]

Many other marvels of science and technology have been enlisted in the service of historical investigation, including using magnetometers for locating shipwrecks;[15] employing computers to decipher ancient writings[16] and to determine astronomical positions in relation to megalithic alignments;[17] utilizing electrical soundings to detect underground structures, and periscope photography to view the insides of hidden chambers;[18] and so on and on.

Unfortunately, however useful have been the applications of science, pseudoscience has not been far behind. Some treasure hunters in Florida, for instance, were offered a "gold-finding machine," while others were offered a magic divining pendulum. (This would swing randomly until—coming over a gold-laden shipwreck—it would allegedly "lock on" the treasure.[19])

Among other examples is the attempt by religious zealots to authenticate the so-called Holy Shroud of Turin. It is an approach in which inexperienced investigators (many of them scientists, to be sure) obviously began with the desired answer and worked backward to the evidence. It is thus a through-the-looking-glass approach, but—even so—it seems less a fairy tale than a tragicomedy.

For more than six centuries the mysterious cloth now known as the Shroud of Turin has raised the question: Is it the actual burial cloth of Jesus? Are its imprints of an apparently crucified man due to natural oils and burial spices, or perhaps even caused by a miraculous burst of radiation at the moment of resurrection? Or is it instead merely a rendering by a clever medieval artist?

The search for an answer begins in the mid-1350s, when the fourteen-foot linen cloth was exhibited at a new little church in northern France. Its owner, one Geoffroy de Charny, claimed it was the true Holy Shroud, and it was depicted as such on a pilgrim's medallion about 1357. But as pilgrims eagerly flocked to see the cloth, a skeptical bishop named Henri de Poitiers launched an investigation.[20]

In a letter of 1389 to Pope Clement VII, Bishop Pierre d'Arcis reported on Henri's investigation. In this, the earliest known written reference to the shroud, Pierre stated:

The case, Holy Father, stands thus. Some time since in this diocese of Troyes the Dean of a certain collegiate church, to wit, that of Lirey, falsely and deceitfully, being consumed with the passion of avarice, and not from any motive of devotion but only of gain, procured for his church a certain cloth cunningly painted, upon which by a clever sleight of hand was depicted the two-fold image of one man, that is to say, the back and the front, he falsely declaring and pretending that this was the actual shroud in which our Savior Jesus Christ was enfolded in the tomb, and upon which the whole likeness of the Saviour had remained thus impressed together with the wounds which He bore. This story was put about not only in the kingdom of France, but, so to speak, throughout the world, so that from all parts people came together to view it. And further to attract the multitude so that money might cunningly be wrung from them, pretended miracles were worked, certain men being hired to represent themselves as healed at the moment of the exhibition of the shroud.

According to d'Arcis's letter, Bishop Henri had been "urged by many prudent persons to take action." Theologians "and other wise persons," he said, had argued that the shroud could not be authentic since the gospels did not mention an imaged shroud. And there was further skepticism "that the fact should have remained hidden until the present time." D'Arcis continued: "Eventually, after diligent inquiry and examination, he [Henri de Poitiers] discovered the fraud and how the said cloth had been cunningly painted, *the truth being attested by the artist who had painted it*, to wit, that it was a work of human skill and not miraculously wrought or bestowed" (emphasis added).[21]

As a result of Henri's investigation, stated Pierre d'Arcis, "The said Dean and his accomplices . . . seeing their wickedness discovered, hid away the said cloth." But it had surfaced once again, prompting Pierre to lay the facts before Clement. "I offer myself here," stated the conscientious bishop, "as ready to supply all information sufficient to remove any doubt concerning the facts alleged" in order to counter "the contempt brought upon the Church" and "the danger to souls." In contrast, Geoffrey de Charny was unable—or unwilling—to say how he had acquired the most significant relic in all of Christendom. (Later his son would claim, vaguely, that it was a "gift," while his granddaughter alleged it was a "spoil of war.")

Clement judged the matter and issued a Bull which, although allowing exhibition of the cloth, ordered that it be advertised only as a copy or "representation." Eventually de Charny's granddaughter, Margaret, gained control of the shroud and, represented by an agent, took it on tour. Apparently she made claims counter to Clement's order, for in Chimay there was another challenge resulting in a minor scandal. Finally, in 1453, although she would be excommunicated for it, Margaret sold the "relic" to the Royal House of Savoy. (Authenticity advocates like to say that Margaret "gave" the shroud to the Duke and Duchess, which is true if we note that in return they "gave" her the sum of two castles.) Subsequently, in 1516 it was depicted in a painting (which provides a useful link in its history) and shortly thereafter, in 1532, the shroud was almost destroyed in a chapel fire, resulting in burn marks and water stains which disfigured the image. And in 1578 it came to rest in Turin.[22]

The modern history of the shroud began in 1898, when it was photographed for the first time. Developing his glass negatives, Secondo Pia was astonished to see that the image's darks and lights were reversed (except for hair and beard), thus demonstrating that the images on the cloth were quasi-negatives. The reported confession aside, proponents argued that the shroud must indeed be authentic, for how could an artist of the Middle Ages have produced "perfect photographic negatives" (as they exaggerated) before the concept of photography?

Indeed, other evidence has been brought forth to argue in favor of authenticity, but—just as surely—critics have challenged it.

Among realistic details supposedly beyond the ken of a forger were flagellation marks on the body image (but medieval paintings depicted contemporary flagellations), nail wounds in the wrists (skeptics insist they are in the base of the palm), and "Roman coins" over the eyes (wishful imagining, say the unconvinced).

Again, shroud proponents argued that the blood flows were amazingly accurate, while skeptics observed they were "picture-like," consistent with an artist's rendering. For example, the distinguished New York pathologist, Dr. Michael Baden, pointed out that the "blood" had failed to mat the hair and instead flowed in rivulets on the outside of the locks. Moreover, the stains are suspiciously still red, in contrast to genuine blood that blackens with age.[23]

Several additional flaws help give the lie to the shroud's authenticity. One is the fact that the print of a foot on the cloth is incompatible with that of the leg it adjoins, another that the hair falls as for a standing (rather than reclining) figure, still another that the physique is so unnaturally elongated (like the figures in gothic art!) that one pro-shroud pathologist concluded Jesus must have suffered from a rare disease known as Marfan's Syndrome.[24]

Artists will readily see the shroud image as essentially traditional, similar to figures from gothic art with some Byzantine influence. As shroud proponent Ian Wilson concedes, "The first consideration was the likeness of Christ that had come down to us in art. Even alone this raised intriguing questions. If the shroud was a forgery, the compatibility was of no special significance because one could presume that the forger merely copied the conventional likeness."[25]

Now the earliest known portrait of Jesus depicted a beardless youth; but eventually the bearded concept prevailed as a matter of rigid artistic convention, as did the location of the lance wound in the *right* side. Only the Gospel of John mentions the piercing of the side and he doesn't specify *which* side, but the shroud image follows the artistic convention.

It does so in other respects. There was a long tradition, dating from the early centuries A.D., of an image of Jesus "not made with hands." Known variously as Veronica's Veil or the Edessan Image or the Mandylion, this was a cloth said to have been impressed with the *facial* image of Jesus *before* the crucifixion. In one account the cloth was said to portray Jesus "from the chest upwards," and by the twelfth century it supposedly showed "the length of his whole body." Like the shroud, the Mandylion image was monochromatic.

Remember, these images were supposedly of the *living* Christ. But there had been numerous "shrouds" as well (some forty by one count), although, until the thirteenth century, these had never been reported as bearing images. As early as the eleventh century had developed the concept of the double-length linen shroud in contrast to the Gospel of John's reference to separate cloths, with one called "the napkin" covering the face of Jesus. These were depicted in certain artistic lamentation scenes. And at this time were also found precedents for the nude, hands-over-the-loins depiction of Jesus like that of the shroud.

The first imaged "shrouds" (merely symbolic ones, with embroidered images) date from at least the thirteenth century. Thus by this time two traditions—represented by blank double-length shrouds on the one hand, and whole-figured nonshroud cloths on the other—had been merged into a single concept: a whole-figured monochromatic shroud.

In 1350, scarcely half a dozen years before the shroud suddenly appeared at Lirey, thousands of pilgrims had been attracted to an exposition in Rome of the Holy Veronica. As Wilson says, "Artists now showed copious bleeding in their renderings of the crucifixion where previously depiction of Christ's blood was restrained or absent altogether." Furthermore, he states, mystics . . . attracted much attention by their lurid and graphic visions of how Christ died, a popular preoccupation intensified by the fact that at this time the Black Death was sweeping Europe. *The climate was therefore exactly right for the appearance of such a macabrely detailed relic of the Passion as the Shroud"* (Emphasis added).26

But Wilson leans strongly toward authenticity. He guesses that the shroud may have been "rediscovered" in some early century and thus have served as a "blueprint likeness" for artists' renderings. Lacking any real evidence, but elaborating on the speculations of an earlier shroud enthusiast, Paul Vignon, Wilson attempts to equate the shroud with the spurious old Edessan Image. Although this bore only a facial image, Wilson supposes that it was really the shroud in disguise, folded in such a way that only the face showed! How to explain the fact that *both* an Edessan Image and a purported burial cloth are mentioned *separately* on certain twelfth and thirteenth-century lists of relics? Why, maybe, Wilson asks us to believe, the "other" Edessan cloth was a *copy* made from the genuine (hypothetically folded) shroud! (Bishop d'Arcis would doubtless find Wilson's scenario—along with the Cloth of Lirey itself—indeed "cunningly painted.")[27]

In 1969, a secret, official commission of experts was appointed to study the purported relic. This fact was leaked to the press, and then denied by Turin church authorities who subsequently had to admit that which they had previously denied. Finally, in 1976, the report of the Turin commission was published.

According to the report, threads were removed from the "blood" areas and subjected to forensic tests, sophisticated tests capable of detecting ancient blood matter and conducted by internationally known experts. However, the "blood" failed all the tests, and the report contained the suggestion that the stains were the result of painting. Two commission members further suggested that the body images had been produced by some *artistic printing* technique, probably employing a model or molds. Many newspaper and magazine articles would subsequently gloss over (or usually omit) much of the commission evidence, while reporting the dubious claim of a criminologist associated with the commission that pollens on the cloth proved its origin in Palestine. The criminologist, Max Frei, actually used no controls and his work was challenged by a Smithsonian botanist. (Just before his death in 1983 Frei suffered a blow to his credibility when, representing himself as a handwriting expert, he pronounced the "Hitler diaries" genuine.)[28]

Further scientific evidence against authenticity came from additional samples removed from the shroud. The Shroud of Turin Research Project (STURP), whose leaders served on the Executive Council of the Catholic Holy Shroud Guild, obtained these samples in 1978, at the time of a new exhibition of the "relic." Sticky tape was used to sample image, "blood," scorch, and off-image areas, and then the tapes were mounted on microscope slides. In all, 32 of the 36 tape samples were submitted to Dr. Walter McCrone of the McCrone Research Institute in Chicago for microscopic and chemical analysis.

Dr. McCrone is one of the world's foremost microscopists, an author of the definitive text, *The Particle Atlas* (1973), and famous for uncovering forgeries. he is uniquely qualified for the task given him. In three reports, published in the journal *The Microscope* and profusely illustrated with photomacrographs and photomicrographs, Dr. McCrone detailed the results of his scientific analyses.[29]

He discovered that *on the image only* were significant amounts of finely powdered ferric oxide "identical in appearance and properties" to a common artist's pigment known as red ocher. In addition, he detected the pigment vermilion, plus trace amounts (suggestive of the shroud's creation in an artist's studio) of orpiment, ultramarine, rose madder, wood charcoal, and azurite (azure blue). All of these pigments had been common in medieval Europe. McCrone determined the "blood" was tempera paint.[30]

Subsequently, STURP turned over the samples to two scientists who eschewed standard tests but nevertheless claimed they had "identified" actual blood. Later, at the 1983 conference of the prestigious International Association for Identification, forensic analyst John F. Fischer explained how results similar to theirs could be obtained with tempera paint, and he demonstrated why spectral data were inconsistent with the STURP scientists' claims.[31] As it happens, neither Heller nor Adler is a forensic serologist or a pigment expert, prompting one to question just why they were chosen for such important work. Heller admitted that McCrone "had over two decades of experience with this kind of problem and a worldwide reputation. Adler and I, on the other hand, had never before tackled anything remotely like an artistic forgery."[32]

An issue more central to the controversy has been the question of image formation. Since the laws of geometry ruled out simple contact imprinting from a body (such images would suffer severe wraparound distortion), and because experiments disproved "vaporography" (the postulated body vapors could produce only a blur), shroud proponents were avowing a miracle, while skeptics were suggesting artistry.

One Los Alamos scientist opined the image was caused by "flash photolysis," that is, a burst of radiant energy, such as Christ's body might have yielded at the moment of resurrection. A shroud enthusiast writing in William Buckley's *National Review* suggested the image was created by thermonuclear reactions and was analogous to laser-produced holograms. And a nun and a Utah chemist concocted a hot-corpse theory: that crucifixion-intensified body heat combined with the alkalinity of a limestone tomb to produce the image through a "mercerization process."[33]

McCrone's tests eventually led him to conclude that the entire image had been painted. In addition to pigments, the shroud image is also composed of a straw-colored stain, which seems to be the predominantly visible element of the tenuous imagery today. Mc-Crone attributed this to a tempera binder, but the samples were taken from him before he had completed his analyses (he says he was "drummed out" of STURP), and in any case he left unexplained why the image stain did not soak into the cloth as the "blood" did. As to the yellow stain, it may merely be the result of cellulose degradation caused by the presence of the foreign substances.[34]

The year previous to STURP's tests, with the encouragement of Paul Kurtz of the Committee for the Scientific Investigation of Claims of the Paranormal (CSICOP), I published results of my successful experiments in simulating the mysterious images. The method—a rubbing technique using a bas-relief sculpture and powdered pigments—automatically yields negative images with numerous points of similarity to the image on the Turin cloth. Among these were minimal depth of penetration, encoded "3-D" information, and numerous other shroudlike features, some of which specifically pointed to some form of imprinting technique. (See Figure 21.)

Shroudologists, however, rushed to dismiss these results on "scientific" grounds. They applied a dubious "image-analyzer test" that succeeded in reassuring devotees, securing favorable media attention for shroud "science," and deflecting attention from the fact that authenticity advocates were themselves bereft of *any* viable hypothesis for the image formation.[35] So consistently different, in fact, have been the ways in which shroud advocates and skeptics have approached the evidence, that the comparison represents a significant lesson to be learned from the extended controversy.

Apart from specific methodological criticisms and the question of competence, the essential difference seems to be one of basic orientation to evidence. Skeptics allowed the preponderance of prima facie evidence—the shroud's lack of historical record before the mid-fourteenth century, the reported forger's confession, the similarities to gothic art, the presence of pigments, and additional clues—to lead them to a conclusion: The shroud is the handiwork of a medieval artisan.

In sharp contrast was the approach of shroudologists who appeared to start with the desired answer and work backward to the evidence. They offered one explanation for lack of provenance

Figure 21. Negative photograph of a rubbing image produced by the author. (Wet cloh was molded to a bas-relief sculpture and, when dry, powdered pigment was applied to prominences.)

(the cloth might have been hidden away), another for the confession (the reporting bishop could have been mistaken), still another for the pigments (an artist copying the shroud could have splashed some on), and so forth.[36]

Evidence for their bias has long been apparent. Months before they had conducted any tests on the cloth, scientists from STURP were making unsubstantiated statements. One said: "I am forced to conclude that the image was formed by a burst of radiant energy— light if you will. I think there is no question about that." Another asserted, "I personally believe it is the Shroud of Christ, and I believe this is supported by the scientific evidence so far." And an Episcopal priest who described his work at a government lab by saying, "I make bombs," testified to the shroud's authenticity: "I believe it through the eyes of faith, and as a scientist I have seen evidence that it could be his [Christ's] shroud."[37]

A further example comes from Air Force scientist Eric Jumper, who was a leader of STURP and a member of the Executive Council of the proauthenticity Holy Shroud Guild. After only a preliminary examination of the "relic" had been made, in 1978, Jumper asserted: "There's no doubt about it—it's a grave cloth!" Soon, arch- conservative Phyllis Schlafly was pronouncing: "At long last we have the proof demanded by the doubting Thomases. This proof is the Shroud in which the body of Jesus was wrapped."[38]

Now, however, to all but entrenched cultists, the issue is settled: The flax from which the linen was made was harvested about the middle of the fourteenth century, about the time an artist reportedly confessed he had "cunningly painted" the image.

The determination that the "shroud" dates from the Middle Ages rather than the time of Christ was officially reported on October 13, 1988, after three laboratories carbon dated postage- stamp-size samples snipped from the Cloth. Using accelerator mass spectrometry, labs at Oxford, Zurich, and the University of Arizona obtained dates in very close agreement: The age span was circa 1260-1390, and the time was given added credibility by correct dates obtained from a variety of control swatches. (These were from the first century B.C. and the eleventh and fourteenth centuries A.D.)[39] The results brought full circle the scientific study of the alleged relic. However, shroud devotees now challenge the implications of the carbon-14 dating tests. While some apparently do not question the medieval date, they agree with the Archbishop of Turin that the imaged cloth is a mysterious icon still suitable for veneration and able to work miracles.[40] Many other shroudologists, particularly those in leadership positions, are refusing to accept the scientific findings, which would be tantamount to admitting they had misled their credulous troops for lo, these many years. As an Episcopal priest who operates a shroud center in Atlanta huffed: "Before it's over, it will be the accuracy of the carbon-14 tests [that are] in question, not authenticity of the shroud."[41]

Many are already calling for new tests. And it seems likely, if we can judge from past actions, that they will want them conducted by loyal shroudologists—perhaps by a pious team of ophthalmologists who have adopted radiocarbon dating as a hobby.

Still others are taking a simpler tack, suggesting that the hypothesized burst of radiant energy at the moment of resurrection (or, alternately, the fire of 1532) changed the carbon ratio. With such a "theory" and a few appropriate calculations, shroud "science" should be able to "correct" the medieval date to a first-century one.

Recommended Works

Ceram, C.W. *Hands on the Past: Pioneer Archaeologists Tell Their Own Story.* New York: Knopf, 1966. Includes much information on application of science to archaeology.

Fleming, Stuart. "Detecting Art Forgeries." *Physics Today* Apr. 1980: 34-39. Overview of sophisticated analyses employed in uncovering forged paintings.

Lauber, Patricia. *Tales Mummies Tell.* New York: Thomas Y. Crowell, 1985. Interesting introduction to scientific examination of mummies.

Mills, John FitzMaurice. *Treasure Keepers.* New York: Doubleday, 1973. Includes chapters on scientific testing, dating, detecting forgeries; intended for the layman.

Nickell, Joe. *Inquest on the Shroud of Turin,* updated ed. Buffalo: Prometheus, 1987. Written with a panel of experts, a skeptical analysis of claims that the "shroud" is the burial cloth of Jesus.

————, with John F. Fischer. "Celestial Painting," chap. 8 of *Secrets of the Supernatural.* Buffalo: Prometheus, 1987, 103-17. Skeptical investigation of the Image of Guadalupe: supposedly a miraculous "self-portrait" of the Virgin Mary, but actually a painted fake.

Some Lessons Learned

The foregoing chapters by no means constitute a complete list of kinds of historical investigation. Another, for example, would be *dating*—determining the age of documents, texts, artifacts, and the like. Still other categories of mysteries readily come to mind. One would be determining relationship, as in the case of the paternity of a man born illegitimate in 1862. One fact, gleaned from a thorough search of county court records—that he had been given an entire farm at age sixteen—seemed to point to the father. So did proof that the grantor had other illegitimate children.[1]

Another example of determining relationship is represented by the 1903 case of "the two Will Wests." They were the criminal lookalikes at Leavenworth Penitentiary whose uncanny resemblance fatally challenged an outmoded identification system and helped launch fingerprinting in America. Although Will West and William West were supposedly unrelated, the author's investigation turned up a body of contrary evidence, which included marked similarities in background, in the names and addresses of siblings on their correspondence records, and in genetically indicative features in their similar fingerprint patterns—evidence that they were, actually, identical twins. In fact, lodged in the old files was a clerk's memorandum reporting how a fellow prisoner had deposed that he personally knew them to be "twin brothers."[2]

A rather unique type of mystery—although related to lost texts (discussed in chapter 8)—occurred in the form of a persistent question among Morgan County, Kentucky, researchers: If the county court records had indeed perished in a courthouse fire during the Civil War (missing, for example, were deed books A through D), why were many *earlier* records still extant? For instance, marriage records were complete from the time of the county's formation in 1823. An inventory of the existing books and a survey of their contents revealed a nearly perfect pattern: Books completely filled at the time of the 1862 fire were destroyed, whereas books in which entries were still being posted had survived. Obviously the latter had been elsewhere—very likely at the clerk's home.[3]

Not only lost texts but other missing historical material invites the services of the investigator. Two examples will suggest the possibilities. One involved a search for three lost ancestral graves: those of a pioneer Kentucky couple and their daughter-in-law. From a long and unbroken tradition, an elderly descendant knew the cemetery and the family plot. Of the three unmarked graves, however, just whose was whose was no longer certain.

The problem was approached logically. Two graves being similarly framed with rough-hewn stones suggested they belonged to the couple. Of those, the early custom of burying the wife at her husband's left side—a custom well verified locally—completed the identification. Tombstones were then erected, hand fashioned and chiseled in imitation of proximate ones from the same era.[4]

The second example concerned a fruitless attempt to locate a photograph of the stately home of the author's great grandfather. Finally, an approach was borrowed from police artists: The house was drawn from the recollections of three elderly women who knew the house well. A photograph of a somewhat similar home was used as a starting point, converted into a pencil sketch, and then modified as necessary. One lady, who had actually lived in the house, was able to visualize each room in turn. Thus it was possible to number and position the windows accurately and—from the location of fireplaces—to project the chimneys. Other persons who had known the house were subsequently able to recognize it from the final pen-and-ink rendering.[5]

Restoring the original interior of an existing house—the only one Abraham Lincoln ever owned—presented researchers with yet a different challenge. They wanted the restoration of the two-story frame house in Springfield, Illinois, to be as accurate as possible. To accomplish this they removed and analyzed samples of paint, pored over the old records of shops where the Lincolns had purchased household goods, and pursued other clues. Stated a National Park Service official: "It's almost like trying to solve a mystery. You have to do a lot of detective work."[6]

Many additional genres could be identified, but those already presented have permitted an overview of historical investigation and have allowed a variety of operative methodologies to be demonstrated. The research on Ambrose Bierce, for instance, in chapter 3—which was inspired by the "coincidental" fact that the missing writer was author of a trilogy, "Mysterious Disappearances," and by serious deficiencies in the generally accepted hypothesis (it is far short of a theory) about Bierce's fate—promoted a preliminary "review-investigation." This involved the gathering of available biographical profiles pertaining to the matter and their analysis from an investigative standpoint: examination of extant hypotheses, weighing of existing evidence, and consideration of various research methodologies and investigative strategies that might warrant a reopening of the case.

The subsequent investigation involved several standard as well as innovative methodologies: assessment of the variant tales about Bierce's alleged Mexican demise (to determine whether they represented a genuine oral tradition), analysis of Bierce's last letters and other evidence as part of a "psychological autopsy" (pertaining to his state of mind in the period before his disappearance), examination of his other writings for clues (and so turning up an essay that considerably strengthened a hypothesis), identification of a notebook entry about Bierce's "last letter," and the attempt to ferret out details of a cover-up (such as the admitted destruction of the letter), as well as other approaches. In general the evidence was pursued in tandem with a working hypothesis to develop what is believed to be the "preferred hypothesis."

The Dickens source-study in chapter 9 utilizes a methodology—similar to motif-comparison by folklorists[7]—to demonstrate the close correspondence of Dickens's passages with accounts of cases he read. A specific technique employed to dramatize the resemblances is a table permitting a side-by-side comparison, analogous to ones used in criminalistics to demonstrate to jurors the similarities of finger impressions and handwriting samples.[8]

In addition, many other techniques and technologies have been described, including chemical and instrumental analyses (employed in testing suspect documents, paintings, and other artifacts); physical experimentation (in replicating a giant Nazca ground drawing and the image on the Turin "shroud"); forensic identification, including matching of ear configurations (used in the case of "Ivan the Terrible"); linguistic analysis (in authenticating Lincoln's Bixby letter); archival research (for example, in seeking alternate sources for lost documents); and numerous others.

Many of the methodologies described either derive from or are parallel to methodologies employed in the forensic sciences and presented in courts of law. As an obvious example, consider how comparing individual characters of old type, so as to identify an early printer, would be comparable to matching typewritten specimens, so as to uncover the author of a ransom note. Such similarity is as it should be, because an investigative approach invites—and actually requires—the gathering of evidence that is as precise and objective as possible, and its presentation toward solving a designated mystery.

In brief, *investigation* applied to historical mysteries has many similarities to investigation in legal matters, beginning with the term itself. Similarities extend to identifiable types of crime such as robbery, homicide, and bunco, as well as to similar and analogous standards of proof. In other words, investigators of whatever variety share a belief that mysteries invite solution, that appropriate methods can be devised to that end, that adequate proof can be an attainable goal, and that a changed—presumably better—view is the ultimate result.

At least it is if we are honest enough to prefer the genuine to the false—and wise enough too.

Notes

1. Introduction

1. For a discussion of historiography, see "Historiography and Historical Methodology," *Encyclopaedia Britannica*, 1980, Macropaedia 8: 945.
2. "Troy, medieval legends of," *Encyclopaedia Britannica*, 1980, Micropaedia 10: 146.   3. *Mysteries of the Ancient World* (Washington, D.C.: National Geographic Society, 1979), 146; "Troy," *New Standard Encyclopedia*, 1982, 13: 415.   4. Ibid.; "Trojan War," *New Standard Encyclopedia*, 1982, 13: 405; John Bowle, *The Concise Encyclopedia of World History* (New York: Hawthorn Books, 1958), 50.   5. *Mysteries*, 146-47.
6. David A. Binder and Paul Bergman, *Fact Investigation: From Hypothesis to Proof* (St. Paul: West, 1984), 162.   7. W.I.B. Beveridge, *The Art of Scientific Investigation* (New York: Vintage, n.d.), 63.   8. Beveridge, 115-16; Elie A. Shneour, "Occam's Razor," *Skeptical Inquirer* 10 (1986): 310-13.   9. Myron G. Hill, Jr., Howard M. Rossen, and Wilton S. Sogg, *Evidence* (St. Paul: West, 1978), 49.   10. In science, a hierarchy exists from "hypothesis" to "theory" to "law"; Beveridge, 64.
11. Martin Gardner, *Fads and Fallacies in the Name of Science* (New York: Dover, 1957),   12. Binder and Bergman, 13.   13. Beveridge, 67-68.   14. John Hathaway Winslow and Alfred Meyer, "The Perpetrator at Piltdown," *Science 83* 4.7 (1983): 33-43.

2. Ancient Riddles

1. Gordon C. Baldwin, *The Riddle of the Past* (New York: Norton, 1965), 68-72.   2. Ibid., 56-57.   3. Ibid., 22-23.   4. Ibid., 17-23, 27-28.   5. *Applied Infared Photography* (Rochester, N.Y.: Eastman Kodak, 1972), 16-17.
6. Geoffrey Bibby, *The Testimony of the Spade* (New York: Knopf, 1956), 37.   7. Ibid., 220ff; H. Robert Morrison, "Megaliths: Europe's Silent Stones," in *Mysteries*, 105.   8. Bibby, 225-26.   9. Bibby, 304-19.
10. Ibid. 194-97; Baldwin, 108ff.
11. Bibby, 316-17; Morrison, 105-109; "Stonehenge," *Encyclopaedia Britannica*, 1980, Micropaedia 9: 586-87.   12. Ron Fisher, "Easter Island: Brooding Sentinels of Stone," in *Mysteries*, 203.   13. Ibid., 198, 201.

14. Erich von Däniken, *Chariots of the Gods?* (New York: Putnam, 1970), ch. 8.   15. Fisher, 211, 213.

16. "Riddles in the Sand," *Discover*, June 1982, 50-57.   17. Von Däniken, *Chariots*, 17.   18. Ibid., 17.   19. Erich von Däniken, *Gods from Outer Space* (New York: Bantam, 1972), 105.   20. Quoted in Loren McIntyre, "Mystery of the Ancient Nazca Lines," *National Geographic*, May 1975, 718.

21. Paul Kosok (written in collaboration with Maria Reiche), "The Markings of Nazca," *Natural History* 56 (May 1947): 201.   22. Von Däniken, *Chariots*, sixth figure following p. 78.   23. Jim Woodman, *Nazca: Journey to the Sun* (New York: Pocket Books, 1977), 37.   24. Ibid., passim. 25. Von Däniken, *Chariots*, 16.

26. William H. Isbell, "The Prehistoric Ground Drawings of Peru," *Scientific American*, October 1978, 140-53; "Solving the Mystery of Nazca," *Fate*, October 1980, 36-48.   27. Isbell, "Prehistoric," 142; "Solving," 45. 28. McIntyre, 716ff.   29. Isbell, "Prehistoric," 150.   30. McIntyre, 725.

31. Simon Welfare and John Fairley, *Arthur C. Clarke's Mysterious World* (New York: A&W Publishers, 1980), 119.   32. Ibid., 131-32.   33. Isbell. 149-50.   34. Frank M. Setzler, "Seeking the Secrets of the Giants," *National Geographic* 102 (1952): 393-404.   35. Welfare and Fairley, 130.

36. "Mystery on the Mesa," *Time*, Mar. 25, 1974, 94.   37. McIntyre, 720.   38. Maria Reiche, *Mystery on the Desert* (1968; rev. ed., Stuttgart: Privately printed, 1976), 44-80.   39. Ibid., 79.   40. Isbell, "Solving," 46.

41. "The Big Picture," *Scientific American*, June 1983, 84.   42. Reiche, 46-47.   43. McIntyre, 724; Isbell, "Solving," 41.

3. Biographical Enigmas

1. The material in this chapter pertaining to authors appeared in Joe Nickell, *Literary Investigation*, doctoral diss., Univ. of Kentucky, 1987, 19-53.   2. Leslie A. Marchand, *Byron: A Biography* (New York: Knopf, 1957), viii-xii.   3. R.W. Griswold, *The Works of the Late Edgar Allan Poe: With a Memoir by Rufus Wilmot Griswold and Notices of His Life and Genius by N.P. Willis and J.R. Lowell*, 4 vols. (New York: Redfield), 1850-58; see Quinn, 639ff. 4. Arthur Hobson Quinn, *Edgar Allan Poe: A Critical Biography* (1941; New York: Appleton, 1942), 639ff.   5. Richard D. Altick, *The Scholar Adventurers* (New York: Macmillan, 1951), 233-34.

6. Richard B. Sewall, "In Search of Emily Dickinson," in William Zinsser, ed., *Extraordinary Lives: The Art and Craft of American Biography* (New York: American Heritage, 1986), 89. See also Rebecca Patterson, *The Riddle of Emily Dickinson* (Boston: Houghton, 1951).   7. Robert A. Caro, "Lyndon Johnson and the Roots of Power," in Zinsser, 218.   8. Ibid.   9. Ibid., 222.   10. Robert Carruthers, *Life of Pope*; cited in *The Home Book of Quotations* (New York: Dodd, Mead, 1967), 159.

11. James G. Randall, "Sifting the Ann Rutledge Evidence," *Lincoln the President*, 2 (New York: Dodd, Mead, 1945), appendix.   12. Fred Goerner, *The Search for Amelia Earhart* (Garden City, N.Y.: Doubleday, 1966), passim.   13. See for example, Shannon Garst, *Amelia Earhart: Heroine of the Skies* (New York: Messner, 1947), 176-80; see also "Amelia Earhart," *New Standard Encyclopedia*, 1982, E-6.   14. Ambrose Bierce, *Can Such Things Be?* (1893; reprint, New York: Albert and Charles Boni, 1924).   15. Nickell, 25-26.

16. Walter Neale, *Life of Ambrose Bierce* (1929; New York: AMS Press, 1969), 429ff.   17. G. Hartley Grattan, *Bitter Bierce*, California ed. (New York: Doubleday, Doran, 1929), 74.   18. Ibid.   19. Bertha Clark Pope, ed., *The Letters of Ambrose Bierce* (1922; reprint New York: Gordian, 1967), 189, 195-98.   20. Ibid., xiv-xvi.

21. Ibid., xvi.   22. Vincent Starrett, *Ambrose Bierce* (1920; Port Washington, N.Y.: Kennikat, 1969), 40.   23. Ibid., 42.   24. Ibid., 42-43.   25. Ibid., 44-45.

26. Ibid., 45.   27. M.E. Grenander, *Ambrose Bierce* (Boston: Twayne, 1971), 74.   28. C.G. Poore, "Ambrose Bierce's Last Tilt with Mars," *New York Times Magazine*, Jan. 1, 1920, 13.   29. E.F. Bleiler, ed., *Ghost and Horror Stories of Ambrose Bierce* (New York: Dover, 1964), x.   30. Grattan, 80-81. At first sight the various accounts of Bierce's alleged Mexican fate might seem to gain some strength from each other. That could indeed be arguable if the stories exhibited the qualities of "true folklore"—including variant texts, oral transmission, *and* traditional form—at the source of which might be anticipated some potential kernel of truth. (See Jan Harold Brunvand, *The Study of American Folklore: An Introduction*, 2d ed. [New York: Norton, 1978], 5-7.) Instead, since the different tales supposedly come from informants who each claimed direct knowledge of the facts, they actually cancel each other. As Fatout suggested, "The various reports make the reader wonder whether Mexican informants might have been playing the Indian game of telling questioners what they wanted to hear" (Paul Fatout, *Ambrose Bierce: The Devil's Lexicographer* [Norman, Okla: Univ. of Oklahoma Press, 1951], 321). Underscoring that possibility is the likelihood that the latter asked leading questions.

31. Starrett, 45-46.   32. Ibid., 31.   33. Grattan, 80. 34. Neale, 437-38.   35. Ibid., 438.

36. Fatout, 317-18.   37. Carol Rudisell, telephone communication, 23 Oct. 1981. I compared the handwriting of the notebook with that of a draft of Carrie Christiansen's letter to "Mr. Neale" of Jan. 31, 1915, a copy of which I received from Stanford University Library.   38. Carey McWilliams, "The Mystery of Ambrose Bierce," *American Mercury* 22 (1931): 330-37. 39. Neale, 439.   40. Ibid., 432-33.

41. Ibid., 430-33.   42. Grattan, 74.   43. Ambrose Bierce, "Taking Oneself Off," in *The Collected Works of Ambrose Bierce* (12 vols., 1909-12; reprint New York: Gordian, 1966), 338-44.   44. Grattan, 74. 45. Fatout, 88.

46. Ibid., 231-32.   47. Bierce in Pope, 164.   48. Grenander,

73.   49. Edmund Wilson, "Ambrose Bierce on the Owl Creek Bridge," *The New Yorker*, Dec. 8, 1951, 164.   50. Bierce in Pope, 198.
    51. Ibid., 195-98.   52. Fatout, 308.   53. McWilliams, 330.
54. Marian Storm, "Discovery," *Forum*, Nov. 1926, 728-37, 764-68.
55. Sibley S. Morrill, *Ambrose Bierce, F.A. Mitchell-Hedges and the Crystal Skull* (San Francisco: Cadleon, 1972), 60ff.
    56. Carey McWilliams, *Ambrose Bierce: A Biography* (New York: Albert and Charles Boni, 1929), 331-33.   57. McWilliams, *Ambrose Bierce*, 326.
58. Frank Edwards, *Strangest of All* (New York: Signet, 1962), 102-103.
59. J. Robert Nash, *Among the Missing* (New York: Simon and Schuster, 1978), 327-32.   60. Bierce, "Taking Oneself Off," 338-39.

4. Hidden Identity

    1. Mark Mayo Boathner III, *Encyclopedia of the American Revolution*, Bicentennial Edition (New York: David McKay, 1974), 968-69; Ann McGovern, *The Secret Soldier: The Story of Deborah Sampson* (New York: Four Winds Press, 1975).   2. Walter B. Gibson, *The Master Magicians* (Garden City, N.Y.: Doubleday, 1966), 104-30; Milbourne Christopher, *Panorama of Magic* (New York: Dover, 1962), 169-71.   3. Joe Nickell, *Morgan County: The Earliest Years* (West Liberty, Ky.: Courier Publishing, 1986), 3.   4. Charles Hamilton and Lloyd Ostendorf, *Lincoln in Photographs* (Norman: Univ. of Oklahoma Press, 1963), 392.   5. Ibid., passim.
    6. Ibid., 64.   7. Richard D. Altick, *The Scholar Adventurers* (New York: Macmillan, 1951), 65-67.   8. Ibid. 67.   9. Ibid., 69-76.
10. Ibid., 76-79.
    11. Mengele attempted plasic surgery (but aborted it midway when he saw the doctor was incompetent) and grew a bushy mustache. See Gerald L. Posner and John Ware, *Mengele: The Complete Story* (New York: McGraw-Hill, 1986), 112-13, 165.   12. Ibid., 309, 319-25.   13. Posner and Ware, 320.
14. Ibid., 325.   15. Ibid., 261.
    16. Allan A. Ryan, Jr., *Quiet Neighbors: Prosecuting Nazi War Criminals in America* (New York: Harcourt, 1984), 1-6, 94-141. See also Milton Meltzer, *Never to Forget: The Jews of the Holocaust* (New York: Harper and Row, 1976) 109-11, 115-16, 145; Robert J. Lifton, *The Nazi Doctors* (New York: Basic Books, 1986), 124, 157, 160.   17. The SS (*Schutzstaffel*) was the elite, fanatical Nazi Security Service led by Himmler.   18. Quoted in Ryan, 96-97.   19. Ibid., 96, 102.   20. Ibid., 105.
    21. Quoted in Ryan, 134.   22. Ibid., 135.   23. "Defense Witnesses 'Self-destruct,' Weakening 'Ivan the Terrible' Case," *Lousiville Courier-Journal*, Aug. 24, 1987.   24. Quoted in Ryan, 133, 136-37.   25. See Joe Nickell with John F. Fischer, *Secrets of the Supernatural* (Buffalo: Prometheus, 1988).
    26. The commander of Demjanjuk's ROA unit testified at his trial. See "J'accuse," *London Sunday Telegraph*, Dec. 13, 1987.   27. Ryan, 100.

28. Patrick J. Buchanan, "Nazi Butcher or Mistaken Identity?" *Washington Post*, Sept. 28, 1986.   29. William E. Smith, "Trial by Bitter Recollection," *Time*, Mar. 2, 1987.   30. Reg Little, "Count Slams Treblinka 'Show Trial,'" *Oxford Times* (England), Apr. 22, 1988.

31. The photograph had been made from very similar angles, and the resulting superimposition was excellent, as illustrated.   32. Lt. Drexel T. Neal and Sgt. Raleigh S. Pate, Lexington-Fayette Urban County Division of Police, Lexington, Ky., personal communication, Aug. 31, 1987.

33. Glenn Taylor, Lexington, Ky., report dated Aug. 25, 1987.   34. See n. 19.   35. Dr. Virginia Smith, Univ. of Kentucky, letter-report to Joe Nickell, Nov. 2, 1987.

36. Alfred V. Iannarelli, letter-report to Joe Nickell, Nov. 14, 1987.

37. Alfred V. Iannarelli, letter to Joe Nickell, Dec. 2, 1987.   38. William Flynn, testimony at trial of Demjanjuk in Isreal (criminal case no. 373/86), Nov. 23-25, 1987, Translators' Pool Ltd. pages no. 10444-727; Flynn, "Demjanjuk Is a Victim of a Soviet Forgery," *Arizona Republic*, July 10, 1988. (There was also a mark on the photo the defense thought might be from a paper clip.)

39. Ibid.   40. Gideon Epstein, trial testimony (see n. 38), May 7, 1987, 5799-5800.

41. Ibid., May 11, 1987, 5873-74.   42. Ryan, 100-2.   43. Undated report, "Technical Proof of the Forgery of the 'Trawniki ID-Card,'" by (name obliterated: a "Senior Research Physicist of the Naval Weapons Center, China Lake, Ca."). Much of the report is an anti-Soviet diatribe.   44. *Langenscheidt's New College German Dictionary* (Berlin: Langenscheidt, 1973), 114. *Bluse* was correctly rendered as "jacket" in an official translation at the Israeli trial, "Exhibit 6 (a)."   45. Buchanan (see n. 28).

46. Gideon Epstein, trial testimony (see n. 40), May 7 and 11, 1987, 5698-5893.   47. Amnon Bezalely, trial testimony (see n. 14), Apr. 21-23, 27, 1987, 4558-5159.   48. Dr. Antonio Cantu, trial testimony (see n. 38), June 25, 1987, 6528-6618.   49. Epstein, Bezalely, and Cantu, trial testimony (see nn. 46-48), passim.   50. Bezalely, 4823ff.

51. Gideon Epstein, "The Trawniki Card: The Role of the Forensic Document Examiner in Modern War Crime Trials," presented to the annual meeting of the American Society of Questioned Document Examiners, Houston, Tex., Aug. 16-20, 1981, p. 2.   52. Epstein, transcript, 5753.   53. Bezalely, 4699.   54. Albert S. Osborn, *Questioned Documents*, 2d ed. (Montclair, N.J.: Patterson Smith, 1978), 332-33.   55. Epstein, transcript, 5840-44.

56. Flynn (see n. 38). Flynn's testimony largely paralleled that of another defense expert, Julius Grant, Nov. 9-11, 1987, 9449-9823.   57. Ibid.

58. "Headline News" report, Cable News Network, Apr. 21, 1988. Recently, documents have come to light that suggest "Ivan" was using the name Ivan Marczenko. Demjanjuk's defenders claim this exonerates him, whereas the Israeli prosecution concludes that the name was a Demjanjuk alias. (The name also appears on his immigration papers as the maiden name of his mother.) See "Demjanjuk Guilt Questioned," *Lexington Herald-Leader*, Dec. 19, 1990.

5. Fakelore

1. Robin W. Winks, ed., *The Historian as Detective* (New York: Harper and Row, 1969), xv.   2. "Oral History," *Academic American Encyclopedia*, 1982, 14: 414.   3. Willa K. Baum, *Oral History for the Local Historical Society*, 2d ed., rev. (Nashville: American Association for State and Local History, 1975), 7.   4. Richard M. Dorson, *American Folklore* (Chicago: Univ. of Chicago Press, 1959), 1-6, 280. The term folklore is also applied to folk creations, such as quilts, and to songs, customs, rituals, all of the inherited traditions of a community.   5. Richard M. Dorson, *Folklore and Folklife: An Introduction* (Chicago: Univ. of Chicago Press, 1972), passim.

6. Ibid., 14.   7. Dorson, *American Folklore*, 232-36. See also Richard Cavendish, ed., *Legends of the World* (New York: Schocken Books, 1982), 334-35, and *The Encyclopedia of American Facts and Dates*, 3d ed. (New York: Thomas Y. Crowell, 1962), 119.   8. *Funk and Wagnall's Standard Dictionary of Folklore, Mythology, and Legend* (New York: Harper and Row, 1972), 848.   9. Dorson, *American Folklore*, 4.   10. Dorson, *Folklore and Folklife*, 313-14.

11. Dorson, *American Folklore*, 4.   12. Joe Creason, *Joe Creason's Kentucky* (Louisville: Courier-Journal and Louisville Times, 1972), 230.
13. Dorson, *American Folklore*, 243.   14. Ibid., 241.   15. "Jewish Myth and Legend," *Encyclopaedia Britannica*, 1980, Macropaedia 10: 191.

16. Lloyd R. Bailey, *Where Is Noah's Ark?* (Nashville: Abingdon, 1978), 83.   17. Gordon Stein, "Noah's Ark: Where Is It?" *Fate*, Feb. 1988, 40-46.   18. See Cavendish, 265-66, for a discussion.   19. "Atlantis," *New Standard Encyclopedia*, 1982, A: 731. It remains possible, of course, that Plato simply made up the tale. (See Cavendish, 262-64.)   20. Dorson (in *Folklore and Folklife*, 14) states, "The resolution of this thorny problem lies in an analysis of each individual tradition according to certain criteria: Have the tradition carriers resided continuously in the same locality, so that visible landmarks reinforce the story live? Does the culture institutionalize oral historians? Are the tribal traditions supported by other kinds of evidence—linguistic, ethnological, documentary—and by external traditions?"

21. Ibid.   22. Dorson, *American Folklore*, 4.   23. Michael Paul Henson, *John Swift's Lost Silver Mines* (Louisville, Ky.: Privately printed, 1975), 8-25.   24. J.H. Kidwell, *Silver Fleece* (New York: Avondale Press, 1927), vii.   25. Lincoln Co. no. 10117, issued May 17, 1788, and filed in the Land Office at Richmond, Va. Copy available from the Land Office in Frankfort, Ky. Reproduced by Henson, 37.

26. Thomas S. Watson, "John Swift's Lost Silver Mines: A Joke?" *State Journal*, Frankfort, Ky., Feb. 22, 1976, 25.   27. Ibid. (citing opinion of Thomas D. Clark, Kentucky historian).   28. Letter of Sept. 26, 1978.
29. *Journal* (Henson's *John Swift's Lost Silver Mines*, 11, 19).   30. In addition to versions cited, there are, for example: Kidwell, 1-8; Henson, *Lost Silver Mines and Buried Treasure of Kentucky* (Louisville, Ky.: Privately printed, 1972), 6-13. There are also numerous unpublished versions.

31. Henson, 8. Henson believes Swift died in Tennessee in 1800 and that

the *Journal* was taken to Pennsylvania and later to Louisville. (See Henson, 7, 40-41.) But if the *Journal* was not circulated until after 1800, how do we explain Filson's treasury warrant of 1788 containing wording which implies Filson possessed a copy?   32. Arthur Hardie Dougherty, "The Legend of the Swifts' and Monday Mine" (sic), undated typescript in the McClung Collection, Lawson McGhee Library, Knoxville, unpaginated. (Doughtery says his brother "procured a very old and faded document from an old man in Virginia by the name of Boatwright," from which the text was transcribed.)   33. Op. cit.   34. By William Elsey Connelley and E. Merton Coulter (Chicago: American Historical Society, 1922), 130-133.   35. *Journal* (Henson), 15. (Cf. Connelley and Coulter, 132.)

36. Ibid., 24-25.   37. Ibid., 14.   38. *Journal* (Henson), 17. Jonathan Swift, the allegorist, was known to early Kentuckians. A creek named "Lulbegrud" (from "Gulliver's Travels") appears on Filson's 1784 map. 39. Henson, 25.   40. Court of Appeals Deed Book A, 307. Aug. 1, 1795.

41. Court of Appeals Deed Book N, 142. Nov. 4, 1809.   42. Henson, 7, 27.   43. Franklin Longdon Brockett, *The Lodge of Washington*, Alexandria, Va., 1899, 127-128.   44. E.g., *William Swyft of Sandwitch and Some of his Descendants*, 1637-1899, compiled by George H. Swift, Millbrook, N.Y.: Round Table Press, 1900.   45. 1788. (Filson's treasury warrant.)

46. 1823. (Judge John Haywood's *History of Tennessee*, 33, 34. Cited by Connelley and Coulter, 115.)   47. 1791. (Fayette Co., Va., Entry Book, 333, in the Kentucky Land Office. Full text of this document is given later in this case study.)   48. 1791. (Ibid.)   49. See examples in Henson, 88-89. 50. *Journal* (Henson), 18.

51. Undated clipping (obtained from Mr. Henson).   52. *Early and Modern History of Wolfe County* (Campton, Ky.: Wolfe Co. Woman's Club, 1958), 13-14. See also *Licking Valley Courier*, Oct. 19, 1978 (West Liberty, Ky.). 53. Op. cit., vii.   54. *Journal* (Henson), 16. The version in *Silver Fleece* (Kidwell, 4) reads "compass square and trowel."   55. *Masonic Heirloom Edition Holy Bible* (Wichita, Ks.: Heirloom Bible Publishers, 1964) 26. (Before proceeding further, let me state that I requested no Mason to compromise himself by revealing society secrets. Data on Masonic symbols and other matters revealed in the following pages are found in encyclopedias and books on Masonry sold to the general public. If I have inadvertently revealed any treasured secrets, that has not been my motive, nor do I intend criticism of Freemasonry in any of my statements.)

56. *Journal* (Henson), 11, 12, 17. Cf. Masonic Bible, 16, 24. Albert G. Mackey (*Symbolism of Freemasonry* [Chicago: Charles T. Powner, 1975], 122) states that Freemasonry is "a science of symbolism."   57. Ralph P. Lester, ed., *Look to the East!* rev. ed. (Chicago: Ezra A. Cook Publications, 1977), 60.   58. *Journal* (Henson), 18.   59. Ibid., 22   60. *Collier's Encyclopedia*, 1978: "Freemasonry." Mackey (315) explains that an allegory is "a discourse or narrative, in which there is a literal and figurative sense, a patent and a concealed meaning; the literal or patent sense being intended by analogy or comparison to indicate the figurative or concealed one." (Curiously, one of Swift's men was named "Guise.")

61. Masonic Bible, 10.   62. Ibid., 26.   62. *Journal* (Henson),
17.   64. Lester, 123.   65. I Kings 10: 27.

66. *Journal* (Henson), 16.   67. Ibid., 22.   68. Lester, 26.
69. Mackey, 190ff.   70. *Journal* (Henson), 16.

71. Masonic Bible, 12, 37, 63.   72. Lester, 150ff.   73. Masonic
Bible, 48.   74. Ibid., 36.   75. Masonic Bible, 1-63. See also Arthur
Edward Waite, *A New Encyclopedia of Freemasonry* (New York: Wethervane
Books, 1970), 1: xiiiff.; Mackey, 313ff.

76. Waite, 1: 367.   77. Henson, *Lost Silver Mines and Buried Treasure of
Kentucky*, 31.   78. Masonic Bible, 50.   79. For further details, see Joe
Nickell, "Uncovered—the Fabulous "Silver Mines of Swift and Filson," *Filson
Club History Quarterly* 54 (Oct. 1980): 337-38.   80. Op. cit., see n. 25.

81. John Filson, *The Discovery, Settlement and Present State of Kentucke* (1784;
rev. ed. New York: Corinth Books, 1962), 25.   82. From Masterson's introduction to *Kentucke*, 1962, VI.   83. *Kentucky Gazette*, Jan. 19, 1787; John
Walton, *John Filson of Kentucke*, Lexington, Ky.: Univ. of Kentucky Press, 1956,
100.   84. *Kentucke*, 58.   85. Ibid., 9.

86. *Journal* (Henson), 11.   87. Walton, 31.   88. *Kentucke*, 11.
89. *Journal* (Henson), 17.   90. Walton, 113.

91. J. Winston Coleman, *Masonry in the Bluegrass* (Lexington, Ky.: Transylvania Press, 1933), 31; Walton, 109.   92. Coleman, 30.
93. Ibid.   94. Walton, 85-86.   95. Ibid., 98.

96. John Bach McMaster, *A History of the People of the United States*, 8 vols.
(New York: D. Appleton, 1883-1913), 1: 516.   97. Walton, 109; Coleman,
Masonry, 31.   98. Ibid., 107-8.   99. Walton, 119-20.   100. Fayette
Co., Va., Entry Book (in the Ky. Land Office), 333.

101. Coleman, 82.   102. Staples, *Pioneer Lexington*, 78.
103. Conneley and Coulter, 113.   104. Ibid.   105. *Kentucke*, 24.

106. "Swift" also termed his group a "company." In the *Journal* (see Henson, 10), he actually places the word in quotation marks. According to *Encyclopaedia Britannica* (1960: "Freemasonry"): the Freemason was "understood
to ba a mason who was free in the sense of being a member of guild or *company*"
(my italics).   107. From a typescript, "Clark Co. Chronicles," in the files of
the Kentucky Historical Society.   108. Willard Rouse Jillson, *Early Clark
County Kentucky: A History, 1674-1824* (Frankfort, Ky.: Roberts Printing, 1966),
65.   109. Beverly W. Bond, Jr., ed., "Dr. Daniel Drake's Memoir of the
Miami Country, 1779-1794," *Quarterly Publication of the Historical and Philosophical Society of Ohio* 18 (1923): 57.

6. Questioned Artifacts

1. John FitzMaurice Mills, *Treasure Keepers* (Garden City, N.Y.: Doubleday, 1973), 6-7.   2. This transcription is based on slightly variant transla-
tions given in Curtis D. MacDougall, *Hoaxes* (New York: Dover, 1958), 110, and
in "Kensington Runestone," *New Standard Encyclopedia*, 1982, 7: 52.
3. MacDougall, 109-11; "Kensington Runestone," 52. See also "Kensington

stone," *Encyclopedia Britannica,* 1980, Micropaedia 5: 761.   4. *The Unexplained: Mysteries of Mind, Space and Time* (New York: Marshall Cavendish, 1984), 6: 795. See also James Randi, *Flim-Flam* (Buffalo: Prometheus, 1982), 128-29.

5. Various forged documents were also created for this purpose; see MacDougall, 194ff.

6. Joe Nickell, *Inquest on the Shroud of Turin,* updated ed. (Buffalo: Prometheus, 1987), 51-52.   7. Ibid., 50ff.   8. Mills, 118-23.   9. Herbert Cescinsky, *The Gentle Art of Faking Furniture* (1931; reprint New York: Dover, 1967), 1.   10. Dora Jane Hamblin, *Pots and Robbers* (New York: Simon and Schuster, 1970), 130-31.

11. Ibid., 141-42.   12. MacDougall, 80-81.   13. Mills, 75-83; MacDougall, 87.   14. Mills, 81, 89-90; Hamblin, 145-50.   15. Hamblin, 68-70.

16. Ibid., 97-98.   17. MacDougall, 83.   18. Mills, 86.
19. Ibid.   20. Ibid., 92; Marian and Charles Klamkin, *Investing in Antiques and Popular Collectibles for Pleasure and Profit* (New York: Funk and Wagnalls, 1975), 39.

21. Klamkin, 146-47.   22. Ibid., 80-81.   23. Ibid., 97.
24. Ibid., 197.   25. Anne Gilbert, *How to Be an Antiques Detective* (New York: Grosset and Dunlap, 1978), 14.

26. Cescinsky, 14.   27. Ibid., 107.   28. M.E. Mason, Jr., letter to Joe Nickell, Apr. 2, 1984.   29. Mills, 87.   30. Robert F. Collins, *A History of the Daniel Boone National Forest, 1770-1970* (Washington, D.C.: U.S. Dept. of Agriculture, Forest Service, Southern Region, 1975); George W. Billings, Jr., "'Historic' Hut Draws Crowds until—," *Lexington Herald* (Lexington, Ky.), Apr. 9, 1968; Glen Adams, "Employee Discovered Site Connected to Daniel Boone, Lost Silver Mine," *LBDA News* (publication of Lexington Bluegrass Army Depot, Lexington, Ky.), May 29, 1984.

31. Bob Rankin, "Dan'l Boone May Have Visited Ky. Cave," *Cincinnati Enquirer,* Apr. 2, 1978.   32. Nevyl Shackleford, "Tantalizing' Find in a Secret Gorge," *Lexington Herald,* Nov. 24, 1967; Billings; Sharon Sherman, "Boone's Burrow?" *Louisville Times,* Apr. 4, 1968.   33. Rankin, "Dan'l Boone."   34. Chip Calloway, "Did Ol' Dan'l Boone Really Sleep There? Tiny Hut Holds Key," *Atlanta Journal and Constitution,* Oct. 25, 1970.
35. George W. Ranck, *Boonesborough,* Filson Club First Publication Series, no. 18 (Louisville, 1901), 111, n. 1.

36. Charles Hamilton, letter to Joe Nickell, Aug. 5, 1983.   37. Lawrence Elliott, *The Long Hunter* (New York: Reader's Digest Press, 1976), 12.
38. John Blakeless, *Daniel Boone: Master of the Wilderness* (New York: William Morrow, 1939), 33.   39. The Boone Letter is in the Durrett Collection, Univ. of Chicago; a copy is in Special Collections, Margaret I. King Library, Univ. of Kentucky (ms. no. 52M48).   40. Draper Papers (Draper Manuscript Collection), State Historical Society of Wisconsin, Series C, vol. 4, 75.5, and vol. 26, 186.

41. Byron Crawford, "Some Odd Bits of History Wind Up in the State Museum's Warehouse," *Louisville Courier-Journal,* Jan. 6, 1982.   42. Shannon Garst, *The Picture Story and Biography of Daniel Boone* (Chicago: Follett, 1965),

70.   43. Ernie Covington, telephone conversation with Joe Nickell, Mar. 26, 1985.   44. Charles Campbell, "Tennessean Positive that Initials on Tree Were Carved by Boone," *Lexington Herald*, Sept. 2, 1977.   45. Henry F. Scalf, *Kentucky's Last Frontier*, 2nd ed. (Pikeville, Ky.: Pikeville College Press, 1972), 435.

46. Louise Rutledge, *D. BOON 1776: A Western Bicentennial Mystery* (Idaho Falls, Id.: Privately printed, 1975).   47. Ibid., 9, 18.   48. Elliott, 12.   49. John Filson, *The Discovery, Settlement and Present State of Kentucke* (Wilmington, Del.: 1784).   50. Calloway, "Did Ol' Dan'l Boone."

51. Bakeless, illus. facing p. 20.   52. Byron Crawford, "Signature on Sandstone Either a Boone or a Bust," *Louisville Courier-Journal*, Mar. 11, 1983.   53. Filson, *Discovery*.   54. F.W. Woolsey, "Seeking New Life for an Old Institution," *Courier-Journal Magazine*, June 24, 1983, 12.
55. Michael A. Lofaro, *The Life and Adventures of Daniel Boone* (Lexington, Ky.: Univ. Press of Kentucky, 1978), 115, 121; Garst, 133-37.

56. Arthur Johnson, *Early Morgan County* (Ashland, Ky.: Economy Printers, 1974), 84; John T. Hazelrigg, Centennial Address, July 4, 1876, in *Licking Valley Courier*, West Liberty, Ky., Dec. 27, 1923.   57. Col. Hazelrigg (1876) said the tree was on the land of Cyrus Perry, Jr., and the 1850 census for Morgan Co., Ky., indicates the Perrys and Blairs lived near each other.
58. Johnson (p. 84) says one tree stood on Smith Creek in Morgan Co. Richard "Dickie" Burks lived on nearby Burks Creek (erroneously given as Birch Creek on some maps), according to Johnson (p. 129).   59. Maria T. Daviess, *History of Mercer and Boyle Counties*, 1 (Harrodsburg, Ky.: Harrodsburg Herald, 1924; reprint 1962), 13.   60. Ibid., 13.

61. Bakeless, 59, 218.   62. Lofaro, 129. A phonetic speller would be more likely to omit the *d* in "frends" than "frend" in final position, since the *d* sound between /n/ and /z/ (-s plural) would be assimilated in speech.
63. See document no. 52W37, Special Collections, Margaret I. King Library, Univ. of Kentucky.   64. Sue McClelland Thierman, "It Says Here: D. Boone, 1793," *Courier-Journal Magazine*, Sept. 29, 1957, 23-27.
65. Ibid.

66. Ibid.   67. Bakeless, 51.   68. Cf. Thierman. See "In the Museum: Daniel Boone's Rifle," *Register of the Kentucky Historical Society* 49 (1951): 166.   69. Hamilton (see n. 36).   70. Our interviewees generally requested anonymity; their names are recorded in our files.

71. John Bivins, letter report to Joe Nickell, Dec. 5, 1984.   72. Mrs. Jennie C. Morton, "Daniel Boone," *Register of the Kentucky Historical Society* 5 (May 1907): 50.   73. Bakeless, 32.   74. William C. Baker (curator of the Tennessee State Museum), letter to William Barrow Floyd, May 9, 1974.   75. For further details see Joe Nickell and John F. Fischer, "Daniel Boone Fakelore," *Filson Club History Quarterly* 62 (Oct. 1988), 457-60.

76. Thomas S. Watson, "Clues Indicate Boone May Still Lie in Missouri," *Louisville Courier-Journal*, June 24, 1983.   77. See Nickell and Fischer, 460.   78. R.C. Koeppen, memorandum report from U.S. Forest Products Laboratory to Lionel R. Johnson, Oct. 26, 1967 (in files of Winchester, Ky., Office of the Daniel Boone National Forest).   79. Billings, "'Historic'

Hut." 80. George W. Billings, Jr., "Builder of 'Boone Hut' Reaffirms Story, But Forest Service Still Investigating," *Lexington Herald,* Apr. 11, 1968. 81. Hugh Catron, telephone conversation with Joe Nickell, Nov. 4, 1984. 82. Troy Catron, Jr., telephone conversation with Joe Nickell, Nov. 4, 1984. 83. Billings, "Builder of 'Boone Hut.'" 84. Eugene Peck, telephone conversation with Joe Nickell, Nov. 4, 1984. 85. Hugh Catron (see n. 81).

86. Martha A. Rolingson, letter report to Robert F. Collins (then supervisor, Daniel Boone National Forest), May 3, 1968. 87. Shackleford, "'Tantalizing' Find." 88. See Nickell and Fischer, 464-65. 89. Bakeless, 12, 314. 90. Ibid., 329.

91. Ibid., 59. 92. Lofaro, 129.

7. Suspect Documents

1. *The Tragedy of King Lear,* 1.2. 2. Curtis D. MacDougall, *Hoaxes* (New York: Dover, 1958), 210. 3. Ibid., 212. 4. Ibid., 212-14. 5. Ibid.

6. Allan Nevins, "The Case of the Cheating Documents: False Authority and the Problem of Survival," chap. 10 of Robin W. Winks, ed., *The Historian as Detective* (New York: Harper and Row, 1969), 198; MacDougall, 197-98; *Encyclopaedia Britannica,* 1960, 7: 127-28, 524-25. 7. MacDougall, 198.

8. Charles Hamilton, *Great Forgers and Famous Fakes* (New York: Crown, 1980), 234-39. 9. Ibid., 195. 10. MacDougall, 84.

11. Hamilton, 100. 12. Ibid., 8. 13. Ibid., 1-37. 14. Nevins, 198. 15. Hamilton, 44-61.

16. Altick, 143. 17. MacDougall, 217. 18. Ibid., 87. 19. Halftone reproductions date from after about 1880. 20. Albert S. Osborn, *Questioned Documents,* 2nd ed. (Montclair, N.J.: Patterson Smith, 1978), 110-15, 273; Hamilton, 267-68.

21. Thomas R. Lounsbury, *The Life and Times of Tennyston* (New York: Russell and Russell, 1962), 64. 22. Robert L. Volz, "Fair Copies and Working Copies," in Edmund Berkeley, Jr., ed., *Autographs and Manuscripts: A Collector's Manual* (New York: Scribner's, 1978), 119; Franklyn Lenthall, "American Theater," in ibid., 477. 23. Roy L. Davids, "English Literary Autographs," in Berkeley, 281. 24. Hamilton, 265. 25. In John G. Nicolay and John Hay, eds., *Complete Works of Abraham Lincoln* (New York: Francis D. Tandy, 1905), 10: 274-75.

26. For the facsimile, see Nicolay and Hay, vol. 3, insert following p. 334. 27. Hamilton, 29, 31. 28. Lincoln's stationery never bore his likeness, but at least one of the facsimiles of the Bixby forgery did: See Sherman Day Wakefield, *Abraham Lincoln and the Bixby Letter* (New York: Privately printed, 1948), 2. 29. Hamilton, 21-23, 29. 30. Ibid., 29.

31. Richard Watson Gilder, introduction, Nicolay and Hay, 1: xxx.

32. Mary A. Benjamin, *Autographs: A Key to Collecting* (New York: Dover, 1986),

124-25.   33. Ibid., 125.   34. Wakefield, 6-7.   35. In Nicolay and
Hay, 6: 288.
      36. Wakefield, 8-9.   37. Ibid., 9-10.   38. Benjamin, 127.
39. William E. Barton, *A Beautiful Blunder: The True Story of Lincoln's Letter to
Mrs. Lydia A. Bixby* (Indianapolis: Bobbs-Merrill, 1926), 63.   40. Quoted in
Wakefield, p. 16; first published in F. Lauriston Bullard, *Abraham Lincoln & the
Widow Bixby* (New Brunswick, N.J.: Rutgers Univ. Press, 1946), 122-28.
      41. Barton, 64-68, 76-78.   42. Ibid., 81-127.   43. Ibid., 29.
44. Ibid., 49.   45. Joe Nickell, *Literary Investigation*, doctoral diss., Univ.
of Kentucky, Lexington, Ky., 1987, 155-61.
      46. Ibid., pp. 60-62, 171. Fred E. Inbau, Andre A. Moenssens, Louis R.
Vitullo, *Scientific Police Investigation* (New York: Chilton, 1972), 40, 53.
47. Benjamin, 140. For a facsimile of the first handwritten draft, see Nicolay
and Hay, vol. 9, insert following p. 208.   48. Nicolay and Hay, 6:
87-109.   49. Professor Pival is coauthor of a number of textbooks, including *The Writing Commitment*, 2d ed. (New York: Harcourt, 1980), coauthor,
Michael E. Adelstein. Recently retired from teaching at the University of
Kentucky, she has long been involved in research in the syntactic structures
used in freshman writing and in the syntax of Doublespeak.   50. Samples
of Lincoln's and Hay's writings were taken from (respectively) the *Complete
Works of Abraham Lincoln* (see n. 1) and *Letters of John Hay and Extracts from Diary*,
vols. 1-3, "Printed but not published, 1908" (New York: Gordian Press, 1969).
      51. See, for example, Joe Nickell, "Discovered: The Secret of Beale's Treas-
ure," *Virginia Magazine of History and Biography*, 90 (July 1982): 310-24.
52. Jean G. Pival, report to Joe Nickell, June 23, 1988.

8. Lost Texts

      1. Richard D. Altick, *The Scholar Adventurers* (New York: Macmillan, 1951),
233-34.   2. Hazel Mason Boyd, *Some Marriages in Montgomery County,
Kentucky, Before 1864* (Lexington, Ky.: Kentucky Society Daughters of the American Revolution, 1961).   3. Morgan was formed from Floyd and, in a lesser
portion, Bath County in 1822-23.   4. For a fuller discussion, see Joe Nickell, *Morgan County: The Earliest Years* (West Liberty, Ky.: Courier Publishing,
1986).   5. See Ada Nisbet, *Dickens and Ellen Ternan* (Berkeley: Univ. of
California Press, 1952).
      6. E. Patrick McGuire, *The Forgers* (Bernardsville, N.J.: Padric Publishing,
1969), 199; Fred E. Inbau, Andre A. Moessens, and Louis R. Vitullo, *Scientific
Police Investigation* (Philadelphia: Chilton, 1972), 61.   7. *Applied Infrared
Photography* (Rochester, N.Y.: Eastman Kodak, 1972), 52.   8. Julius Grant,
Books and Documents: Dating, Permanence and Preservation (New York: Chemical
Publishing, 1937), 1122.   9. George Martin Cunha and Dorothy Cunha,
Conservation of Library Materials, 2d ed. (Metuchen: Scarecrow, 1971), 1: 343;
Grant, 85. Portable ultraviolet lamps can be purchased and can be most useful
to the serious genealogist or other person confronted with faded ink.
10. Grant, 86.

11. McGuire, 191.   12. Altick, 201.   13. Allan Nevins in Robin W. Winks, ed., *The Historian as Detective* (New York: Harper and Row, 1969), 211-12.   14. Willard Rouse Jillson, *Filson's Kentucke* (Louisville, Ky.: J.P. Morgan, 1930), 179.   15. Lincoln County, Va., treasury warrant no. 10117, issued May 17, 1788, and filed in the Land Office at Richmond, Va.; copy available from the Kentucky Land Office in Frankfort, Ky.

16. Oscar Ogg, *The 26 Letters* (New York: Crowell, 1948), 45-49.
17. "Cuneiform," *Encyclopaedia Britannica*, 1973, 6: 898.   18. Altick, 206-9.   19. Millar Burrows, in Winks, 257-71.   20. Christopher Morley, in Winks, 89-103; Altick, 16-36.

21. Edward H. Cohen, *Ebenezer Cooke: The Sot-weed Canon* (Athens, Ga.: Univ. of Georgia Press, 1975), 46.   22. The title page reads: "THE/*Sot-weed Factor:* / Or, a Voyage to / MARYLAND. / A/SATYR. / In which is describ'd, / The Laws, Government, Courts and / Constitutions of the Country; and also the / Buildings, Feasts, Frolicks, Entertainments / and Drunken Humours of the Inhabitants of / that Part of America. / In Burlesque Verse. / By Eben. Cook, Gent. / LONDON: / Printed and Sold by *B. Bragg*, at the *Raven* in *Pater-Noster-Row*. 1708. (Price 6*d*.)" / A copy is owned by the Library of Congress. (John Shawcross has called my attention to the fact, previously unrecorded by others, that *The History of the Works of the Learned*, vol. 9 for December 1707, p. 756, records as published: "The Sot-weed Factor; or, Voyage to *Maryland;* a Satyr. By *Eben Cook*, Gent. Sold by *B. Bragg*." A copy is in the William Andrews Clark Library.)   23. James D. Hart, *The Oxford Companion to American Literature* (New York: Oxford Univ. Press, 1965), 180; Max J. Herzberg, *The Reader's Encyclopedia of American Literature* (New York: Thomas Y. Crowell, 1962), 206; Philip E. Diser, "The Historical Ebenezer Cooke," *Critique: Studies in Modern Fiction* 10.3 (1968): 48-50.   24. The title page reads: "THE / MARYLAND MUSE. / CONTAINING / I. The History of Colonel NATHANIEL BACON'S Rebellion / in VIRGINIA. Done into *Hudibrastick* Verse, from / an old MS. / II. The SOTWEED FACTOR, or Voiage to *MARYLAND*. / *The Third EDITION, Corrected and Amended.* / By E. COOKE, Gent. / *Let Critics that shall discommend* it, / ————————————*mend* it. / [type device] / *ANNAPOLIS:* / Pinted in the Year, M,DCC, XXXI." The British Library has the only known copy.
25. For the text of the drafts, see Cohen 47-49. The volume is located in the Hall of Records in Annapolis.

26. The Bordley elegy (mentioned earlier) is Parks's first literary publication.   27. Cohen, 52.   28. Ibid., 59.   29. The title page (see n. 24) shows that the work was published at Annapolis, and as Bernard E. Steiner observed (in his *Early Maryland Poetry*), "William Parks is the only printer commonly supposed to have been there in 1731" (quoted in Cohen 101). Also, Parks published the Bordley elegy and the *Sotweed Redivivus*.   30. The title page reads: "*SOTWEED REDIVIVUS:* / Or the PLANTERS / Looking-Glass. / In burlesque Verse. / Calculated for the Meridian of / *MARYLAND*. / by E. C. *Gent*. / *Non-videmus, id Manticae quod in Tergo est*. Juv. / ANNAPOLIS: / Printed by WILLIAM PARKS, for the Author. / M.DDC.XXX." A copy is owned by the New York Public Library.

31. Cohen, 58.   32. James T. Pole, "Ebenezer Cook: *The Sot-weed*

Factor, Edited with Photostatic Text," thesis, Columbia Univ., 1931, 138-42.
33. Published in 1654; 1st ed., 1641, entitled, *An Answer to a Book*. For this important observation I am indebted to John T. Shawcross.   34. This is entirely possible since we have only single copies of many colonial works, including Cooke's *The Maryland Muse*. If, however, it were supposed the "second edition" was published in England, surviving copies would be more likely.   35. Cohen, 24.

9. Obscured Sources

1. Arthur Pierce Middleton and Douglas Adair, "The Mystery of the Horn Papers," *William and Mary Quarterly*, 3d ser., 4 (Oct. 1947): 409-43; reprinted (in slightly abridged form) in Winks, 142-69.   2. Ibid., 160-61.   3. Ibid., 168.   4. The anecdote appeared in the fifth edition, 1806; it is reproduced, for example, in Ralph Henry and Lucile Pannell, ed., *My American Heritage* (New York: Rand McNally, 1949), 166-67.   5. Curtis D. MacDougall, *Hoaxes* (New York: Dover, 1958), 106-7.

6. *Louisville Daily Courier*, November 1, 1853.   7. Negley K. Teeters, *Hang by the Neck* (1967); cited in Joe Nickell, *The Peddler Legend: Murder and Hanging in Morgan County, Kentucky, 1852-53* (West Liberty, Ky.: Nickell Genealogical Books, 1988), 13.   8. R.W. Stallman, "The Scholar's Net: Literary Sources," *College English* 17 (1955): 23.   9. G.B. Harrison, ed., *Shakespeare: The Complete Works* (New York: Harcourt, 1952), 270, 774, 880, 1136.
10. Samuel Copp Worthen, "Poe and the Beautiful Cigar Girl," *American Literature* 20 (1948): 306.

11. Richard D. Altick, *The Art of Literary Research* (New York: Norton, 1975), 281.   12. J. Cuming Walters, "Dickens and Captain Marryat," *Dickensian* 14 (1918): 267; Elizabeth Wiley, "Four Strange Cases," *Dickensian* 58 (1962): 120-25.   13. Ibid., 122.   14. Trevor Blount, "Dickens and Mr. Krook's Spontaneous Combustion," *Dickens Studies Annual* (1970): 184-90.
15. *Gentleman's Magazine* 16 (1746): 368; extract in the *Dickensian* 32 (1936): 151. For a skeptical discussion of the Bandi case and other alleged instances of "spontaneous human combustion," see chapter 11 and the appendix of Joe Nickell with John F. Fischer, *Secrets of the Supernatural* (Buffalo: Prometheus, 1988), 149-57, 161-71.

16. Altick, 16.   17. Theodric Romeyn Beck and John B. Beck, *Clements of Medical Jurisprudence*, 5th ed., 2 vols. (Albany, N.Y.: O. Steele et al., 1835) 2: 62.   18. Newton Arvin, ed., *The Heart of Hawthorne's Journals* (1929; New York: Barnes, 1967), 68-77; James Playsted Wood, *The Unpardonable Sin: A Life of Nathaniel Hawthorne* (New York: Pantheon, 1970), 68-72; Arlin Turner, introduction to Nathaniel Hawthorne, *The Blithedale Romance* (New York: Norton, 1958), 9-11.   19. Turner, 11-12.   20. Ibid., 12.

21. Arvin, 82; Turner, 12-13.   22. John Gatta, Jr., "Aylmer's Alchemy in 'The Birthmark,'" *Philological Quarterly* 57 (1978): 399-413.
23. *Blithedale*, 204.   24. Milbourne Christopher, *Panorama of Magic* (New York: Dover, 1962), 42, 57-62.   25. Ibid., 19, 27, 46; Professor Hoffman

(Angelo John Lewis), *Modern Magic: A Practical Treatise on the Art of Conjuring* (1876; Philadelphia: David McKay, n.d.), 312.
    26. Christopher, 80-88.   27. Ibid., 70.   28. *Blithedale,* 45, 111, 196-97.   29. Ibid., 209.   30. Ibid., 55.
    31. Nathaniel Hawthorne, *The House of Seven Gables* (1851; New York: J.H. Sears, n.d.), 25.   32. *Blithedale,* 205.   33. Ibid., 126.   34. Ibid., 129.   35. Ibid., 133.
    36. Ibid., 210.   37. Ibid., 197.   38. Ibid., 127.   39. Ibid., 34.   40. Ibid., 207.
    41. Christopher, 63.   42. Henry Hay, ed. *Cyclopedia of Magic* (Philadelphia: David McKay, 1949), 313-16.   43. Edwin A. Dawes, *The Great Illusionists* (Secaucus, N.J.: Chartwell, 1979), 147.   44. Christopher, 62.   45. The letter is reproduced in abridged form in Arvin, 84-86.
    46. Turner, 14.   47. Ibid., 6.   48. For a discussion, see Joe Nickell, *Literary Investigation,* doctoral diss., Univ. of Kentucky, 1987, 78-80.
49. *Blithedale,* 27.   50. For a further discussion along similar lines, see Frederick C. Crews, "A New Reading of *The Blithedale Romance,*" *American Literature* 29 (1957): 147-70. He observes, for example (p. 155), that "Coverdale's aristic ideal is marriage of actual life with an ennobled taste. Real people must be the subject of his romance, but they must give forth 'an indescribable ideal charm.'"

10. Scientific Challenges

    1. John FitzMaurice Mills, *Treasure Keepers* (New York: Doubleday, 1973), 28, 78, 91-92, 95; Stuart Fleming, "Detecting Art Forgeries," *Physics Today,* April 1980, 37.   2. Charles E. O'Hara, *Fundamentals of Criminal Investigation,* 3d ed. (Springfield, Ill.: Charles C. Thomas, 1973), 719-23; Mills, 24, 29.
3. Mills, 31.   4. Ibid., 29-31.   5. Ibid., 25, 31-34, 85.
    6. *Applied Infrared Photography* (Rochester, N.Y.: Eastman Kodak, 1972), 36-38, 52.   7. Ibid., 16-17.   8. Mills, 28-29.   9. John F. Fischer and Joe Nickell, "Laser Light: Space-age Forensics," *Law Enforcement Technology,* September 1984, 26-27.   10. Mills, 39-45.
    11. *The Young Christ* is also known as *Jesus among the Doctors;* see Piero Bianconi, Appendix: "Fake Vermeers and the Van Meegeren 'Affair,'" *The Complete Paintings of Vermeer* (New York: Harry N. Abrams, 1967), 101.
12. Mills, 76-77.   13. Bianconi, 100-102; Mills, 75-83; Curtis D. MacDougall, *Hoaxes* (New York: Dover, 1958), 87.   14. "3, 400-year-old Mummy Gets Face Lift in Louisville," *Lexington Herald-Leader,* June 25, 1989; Robert Kaiser, "Anthropologist Gives Mummy a New Face," ibid., July 11, 1989.   15. Kip Wagner, as told to L.B. Taylor, Jr., *Pieces of Eight: Recovering the Riches of a Lost Spanish Treasure Fleet* (New York: E.P. Dutton, 1966), 140.
    16. C.W. Ceram, ed., *Hands on the Past* (New York: Knopf, 1966), 416-20.   17. *Mysteries of the Ancient World* (Washington, D.C.: National Geographic Society, 1979), 105-9, 120. The reference is to the controversial work of Gerald S. Hawkins.   18. Carlo Maurilio Lerici, "The Lerici Periscope,"

in Ceram, 407-12.　　19. Wagner, 173.　　20. Joe Nickell, "in collaboration with a panel of scientific and technical experts," *Inquest on the Shroud of Turin*, updated ed. (Buffalo: Prometheus, 1987), 12ff. Except as noted, this is the source for information in the remainder of the chapter.

21. Ibid., 13.　　22. Ibid., 13-27.　　23. Ibid., 57-75, 77ff. 24. Ibid., 71. See also "Shroud Reveals Lincolnesque Disease," *New Orleans Times-Picayune*, Jan. 31, 1982.　　25. Ian Wilson, *The Shroud of Turin*, rev. ed. (Garden City, N.Y.: Image books, 1979), 98.

26. Ibid., 201-202.　　27. Ibid., 119-21.　　28. Nickell, 109-14, 128-29, 151-52.　　29. Walter C. McCrone, "Light Microscopical Study of the Turin 'Shroud,'" *The Microscope* 28 (1980): 105-13, and 29 (1981): 19-38.　　30. Nickell, 119-40.

31. See also John F. Fischer, "A Summary Critique of Analyses of the 'Blood' on the Turin 'Shroud,'" in Nickell, 157-60.　　32. John Heller, *Report on the Shroud of Turin* (New York: Houghton Mifflin, 1983), 168.　　33. Nickell, 87, 93, 152.　　34. Ibid., 133-40.　　35. Ibid., 88-91. The "image-analyzer test" supposedly proved the shroud had unique "3-D" properties, but the methodology involved a series of questionable "corrective" factors necessary for visually pleasing results. In any case, experts at a textile lab reportedly obtained comparable results for a simulated shroud image, as demonstrated on a program on the shroud aired on the Discovery channel, July 31, 1987. See also Joe Nickell, "Unshrouding a Mystery: Science, Pseudoscience, and the Cloth of Turin," *Skeptical Inquirer* 13.3 (Spring 1989): 297-98.

36. Wilson, 136; Kenneth E. Stevenson and Gary R. Habermas, *Verdict on the Shroud* (Ann Arbor, Mich.: Servant Books, 1981), 104; Heller, 212. 37. Quoted in Nickell, *Inquest*, 115.　　38. Ibid., 114-15; Phyllis Schlafly, "Proven by Shroud of Turin, 'The Most Remarkable Miracle in History,'" *St. Louis Globe Democrat*, Dec. 13, 1979.　　39. P.E. Damon et al., "Radiocarbon Dating of the Shroud of Turin," *Nature* 337 (1989): 611-15.　　40. Roberto Suro (New York Times News Service), "Church Says Turin Shroud Not from Christ's Burial," *Lexington Herald-Leader*, Oct. 13, 1988.

41. Quoted in Philip J. Hilts, "It's 14th-century, Say the Labs," *Washington Post National Weekly Edition*, Oct. 3-9, 1988.

11. Afterword

1. This was a genealogical case the author investigated.　　2. Joe Nickell with John F. Fischer, "Double Trouble: Synchronicity and the Two Will Wests," chap. 6 of *Secrets of the Supernatural* (Buffalo: Prometheus, 1988), 75-88.　　3. Joe Nickell, "Our Nation's Heritage Prompts a Look at Our Local Heritage," *Licking Valley Courier* (West Liberty, Ky.), July 5, 1984. Also surviving were the entire set of survey books, believed to have been in the custody of the county supervisor.　　4. The graves were those of the author's great, great, great, great grandparents, John Nickell (1771-1849) and Elzy (Wilson) Nickell (1768-1851), and his great, great, great grandmother, Rachel (Kash) Nickell (1794-1853). They are located in the Holderby Graveyard, near

Hazel Green, Wolfe Co., Ky. The informant was the late Milton C. Nickell.   5. The home was the West Liberty, Ky., residence of Attorney John B. Phipps (1860-1929) and his wife, Allie Jo (McGuire) Phipps (1864-1920). Assisting with the reconstruction were Bessaleen Resch, Ivis W. Terrell, and the author's mother, Ella T. Nickell.

        6. Larry Blake, the National Park Service's site chief for visitor services, quoted in William Stracener, "$2.2 million spent to fix Lincoln's $1,500 Home," *Lexington Herald-Leader*, Mar. 28, 1988.   7. Linda Degh, "Folk Narrative," in Richard M. Dorson, *Folklore and Folklife: An Introduction* (Chicago: Univ. of Chicago Press, 1972), 60.   8. Fred E. Inbau, Andre A. Moenssens, and Louis R. Vitullo, *Scientific Police Investigation* (Philadelphia: Chilton, 1972), 40, 53.

Index

DATE DUE

DEMCO 38-296